"Entertaining *and* educational! 'Beloved School Horses' is a must-read for all horse or animal lovers. Sharon Miner writes with a spirit and wisdom that makes it a fun ride all the way."

— *Cathi W., San Francisco, CA*

"Blessed are the broodmares and the school horses. A terrific read."

— *Lee Lyons,*
Windfield Morgans, Litchfield, CT

"Kids and horses meet each other heart to heart. It's not about size, or beauty or price tag. Sharon Miner's stories capture the essence of that heartfelt connection - having a best friend you can depend on."

— *Lauren Quintana,*
Mountain Laurel Riding Stable, White Haven, PA

"These are fun and uplifting stories. It was emotional for me because I grew up with, and later taught with, some of these very special horses."

— *Jessica Seman, former student and*
instructor at Unicorn Stables, Salisbury, MD

"Everyone that reads this book is going to see some of themselves in it and also recall memories of when they were learning about horses. More importantly, it demonstrates what magnificent animals horses are and what has attracted us to them."

— *Bruce Rapport, Associate Dean &*
Hospital Director, University of Pennsylvania
New Bolton Center, Kennett Square, PA

"Someone has finally done it! Not since Anna Sewell's 'Black Beauty' have I read a children's story about horses that is also educational. Sharon has skillfully added into her short stories many details explaining horse care and important safety issues. I really liked how she subtly added these details…Sharon's characters set good examples of how a horse person would act in certain situations. Overall, the stories were very entertaining."

"Neat stories. Good school horses are priceless and will go straight to heaven."

"These unique stories are entertaining and educational, and a great tribute to great horses."

"A fun trail ride down memory lane reminding us of the many wonderful horses who taught us about riding, friendship and life."

"Captivating stories for all horse enthusiasts."

Beloved School Horses
By
Sharon Miner

Illustrations By
Martina Davidova

ISBN 0-7414-2225-5

Copyright for Sharon Miner, www.sharonminer.com

Cover design by Joshua Miner, www.joshuaminer.com

Illustrated by Martina Davidova

Published by:

INFINITY
PUBLISHING.COM

1094 New DeHaven Street, Suite 100
West Conshohocken, PA 19428-2713
Info@buybooksontheweb.com
www.buybooksontheweb.com
Toll-free (877) BUY BOOK
Local Phone (610) 941-9999
Fax (610) 941-9959

∞

Printed in the United States of America

Printed on Recycled Paper

Published September 2004

In memory of my dad, William R. Bach

He believed in me,
and my dream to teach riders on beloved school horses.

~ * ~

Also, in memory of Earl Harker

A fantastic friend and a fantastic resource
for great lesson horses and ponies.

Introduction

As a little girl growing up in Connecticut, I begged my daddy to find horses while we were taking our Sunday drives in the country. I was the middle child of eleven, and often our Sunday entertainment was visiting state parks and beaches, or other outdoor recreational areas. I remember Dad found a herd of ponies that would approach the fence where I stood holding grass. It was such a thrill to have them eat out of my hand, and sometimes they let me pet them. I would not wash my hands that night, so I could smell the delicious aroma until I fell asleep.

When I was 11 years old, I wrote on a piece of paper that in ten years I would own a stable with Quarter Horses, Morgans and Arabians. I would live in Vermont, Pennsylvania or Maryland. I may or may not be married, and may or may not have children. When you are eleven, that isn't important. I reached my goal at 21 years of age, living in Pennsylvania with my husband and five stepsons. I still have that piece of paper.

My oldest sister, Meri, introduced me to trail riding, but the stable sent out unguided rides. I remember for my 12th birthday she took me there with her friends. When we arrived at the first grassy meadow, she rode off with the others while I sat on a huge horse that contentedly ate an afternoon snack. I knew nothing about controlling this magnificent beast, so after a few attempts at pleading with him unsuccessfully, I was resigned to just sitting in the big Western saddle, enjoying the horse's company. After awhile, the animal decided it was time to go home. With a loud neigh, he turned and ran for the barn while I clung to the saddle horn, exhilarated with the speed.

I was determined to learn more, and not just from books which were plentiful in my house as my mom worked at the library. I saved my money earned from babysitting and offered to work at stables in exchange for riding.

I was fortunate to find Lee's Riding Stable, then located in Wilton, Connecticut, where I learned to ride bareback. When I was 15 years old, I purchased my first horse – a black weanling colt I named Charcoal. He died before he was a year, but I didn't give up my dream. I graduated as a junior from high school so I could move with the stable to Litchfield, and I soon bought other horses.

I achieved my goal when I was 21 years old. I was teaching children on a special horse I raised, named Fawn. As interest grew, I acquired a buckskin gelding, Knipper, and Mr. Ed, a small white pony. Unicorn Stables was formed in 1975 in Langhorne, Pennsylvania.

That same year, I married Bob, a wonderful man who supported my dream. The deal was that I would help raise his five sons – 5 years old to 15 – and he would accept my love of horses. The boys all grew up and left home eventually, but horses are still a very large part of our life.

For three years we lived in Langhorne's old farmhouse, a haunted house, but that's another story. Unicorn Stable grew and we moved to Salisbury, Maryland where we expanded to up to forty lesson horses and boarders. We attended small horse shows and held open shows for the local riders. It was a family-oriented barn with special events such as Hay Parties (cookouts after gathering and storing the baled hay), Halloween Horse Show and Haunted Barn Maze (my son designed with his school friends for several years), Beach Rides at the Atlantic Ocean in Delaware, Picnic Trail Rides, and Trail Rides to the Salisbury Zoo. In the summer we held Unicorn Stable's Summer Day Camp.

From 1988 until 1999, I was also the summer Riding Director at Lake Bryn Mawr Camp in Honesdale, Pennsylvania, where several stories take place. In 1996, we sold our farm in Salisbury for a smaller one in Honesdale. During the four years there, I taught girls at Camp Perlman as well as local children.

We closed Unicorn Stables in 2000. I pursued my writing career by working in corporate environments, but I still needed to smell horses. So I worked at Mountain Laurel Riding Stable in the Poconos as a trail guide, and later at Grier School, a private girl's boarding school in Tyrone, Pennsylvania.

I love sharing my love of horses with others, and now this book helps me accomplish that goal. These horses are only twenty of the most revered. Fawn began my interest in writing about horses, and she is so near and dear to my heart that she will have her own book someday.

These stories are told to the best of my recollection. Only first names are used and many are fictitious. Although some of the stories are dramatized, they are all based on true incidents.

Many thanks to these horses and riders for all the fond memories.

Many, many thanks to Lee for being my mentor and friend for more than 35 years, as well as giving me the opportunity to know so many wonderful school horses, some of whom went home with me.

I also thank my son, Josh, for not only the cover designs, but also all the help he gave me at Unicorn Stables.

And I thank Martina for her fabulous sketches drawn from old, not-so-great photos.

But most of all, I thank my husband, Bob, for without his help, there would never have been Unicorn Stables. And thanks to his son, Rick, who helped build the barn in Salisbury.

Last, but not least, I thank my parents for always supporting my dreams.

Happy Trails!

Sharon Miner

Table of Contents

Beloved School Horses

Chapter 1

Farewell and the Girl Scout

I watched the five young girls exit the minivan and march excitedly toward me as I stood at the entrance to my barn. They were of various sizes and hair color, but all smiled or giggled except one youngster. The littlest girl looked scared to death.

They were Girl Scouts and they were working on their Horse Lover's badge. I welcomed the troop and their leader. We introduced ourselves and I learned that the shy girl was Janelle. I gave them a tour of the stable and showed them the horses. As I reviewed the safety rules and fitted them for riding helmets, I evaluated their personalities. I knew I would have Janelle ride Farewell, my aged dark chestnut Morgan horse. It would be a challenge to have her overcome her fear of the unknown, and Farewell was the perfect match to help me achieve my goal.

I had the girls sit on a bench while I led Farewell out of his stall. Standing in front of the girls, I explained the basic parts of the horse and equipment.

"Horses have their own language," I continued after showing them the reins, stirrups and girth. "Does anyone know what it means when a dog wags its tail?"

"It means he's happy!" The tallest girl was very confident.

"That's right. What does it mean when a horse wags his tail?"

"He's happy?" The tall girl wasn't so sure now.

"No, it means he's chasing flies! Do you know what a horse does when he's happy? He blows his nose! And this

1

horse is special because he always blows his nose when he's ridden. That means he's happy and he likes you!"

All the girls giggled except for Janelle who clutched the seat of the bench. She would need more information to convince her to climb up on one of these strange beasts.

"This is Windfield Farewell and before anyone can ride, you have to hear his story. Farewell is the smallest horse you'll be riding today. He is actually a large pony standing at 14.1 hands from the top of his withers to the bottom of his hoof. He is a Morgan horse and Windfield is the name of the Morgan horse farm in Litchfield, Connecticut where he was born.

"He was named Farewell after the two veterinarians who saved his life. When his mother, Wendy, was pregnant with him, she was attacked by wild dogs and almost died. On that day, Wendy gave birth to her son a month early and that is why he is much smaller than his mother or father. Doctor Ferris Gorra and Doctor Paul Elwell saved Wendy's life and her newborn son. So the owner named the colt Farewell in honor of them.

"I brought Farewell home when he was weaned at about four months of age. I trained him and, when he was ready, I showed him at Dressage horse shows. It was the only type of show that didn't give him bad scores for being small. He was a stallion until he was eleven and has fathered several foals. Stallions are daddy horses and not good for children to ride. Just like when cats and dogs are spayed so they can't have babies, boy horses are gelded and that also makes them very gentle. After Farewell was gelded, he became our best-trained lesson horse. Farewell is the sweetest and quietest of all our horses."

My eyes were on Janelle. She was staring at Farewell and seemed a little less afraid.

"Since he's an old boy now, only small children are allowed to ride him. Let's see. I think Janelle can have that privilege today."

Janelle gave a hint of a smile and I assigned the other girls their horses. With an assistant, I had the girls mount and form a circle around me. We showed them the correct position for their seat and legs on the Western saddles, and how to hold the reins in one hand. For balance and to keep her back straight, I had each girl hold the back of the saddle with her other hand.

"Just like any game, you have to know the rules before you can play. The horses already know them so you just have to remind them of the rules. There are four simple things for you to remember so that your horse will listen to you. And if you make a mistake, do you know what will happen?"

The oldest girl shook her head. Janelle's eyes became as wide as donuts and her hand held the saddle in a death grip.

"Your horse will stop in the middle of the ring and fall sleep!"

Even Janelle relaxed then and giggled with the other girls.

"The four things you have to remember are the four aids, or the parts of your body that tell the horse what to do. The signals you give, if done correctly, are like pushing buttons on a video game. Can anyone guess what part of your body gives the horse a signal?"

"Your hands?"

"Good guess, Janelle!" I was pleased that her fears were melting away.

We reviewed the four natural aids – hands, legs, seat and voice – and how to use them to control the horse. My assistant walked next to the first mount and I put the other

3

horses in a single file behind them, a horse distance apart. Janelle and Farewell were last in line as the aged gelding walked slower than the others. After the first time around the ring, practicing walking and stopping, Janelle relaxed even more. When I asked if they wanted to keep going, they all exuberantly agreed.

We practiced some turns, and when they looked balanced and in control, I had them try short trots one at a time. I stayed next to Farewell watching Janelle for a reaction.

As we jogged down the side of the ring, Farewell blew his nose in contentment.

"See, Janelle? Farewell's having fun! He likes you!"

Janelle rewarded me with a pumpkin-size grin.

"When we come back to finish our badge," she whispered seriously when we halted. "Can I ride Farewell?"

"Of course you can!"

Windfield Farewell, my confidence booster, had done it again.

Windfield Farewell - The Rest of the Story

In 2004, at 28 years of age, Farewell retired after teaching beginner walk/trot lessons at Apple Brook Farm in Cookstown, New Jersey for a year. He and his best buddy, Sonny, are enjoying the leisure lifestyle they deserve after so many years of service to children and adults.

His sire, Oakwood's Ethan (fondly known as Studley) and dam, Wendy Allen, lived into their early thirties as Morgans often do.

When Farewell was a young stallion, I showed him in Western and English Pleasure classes at local open horse shows. We even entered a Jousting show on a whim and he won a trophy for spearing rings. But it was Dressage that he excelled at and he learned to get on the bit, collect and extend his strides, and leg yield. We competed through First Level and sometimes entered Combined Tests, which included a Dressage test and stadium jumping. He didn't care for the obstacles and tended to bunny-jump them.

As I became more interested in Eventing (Combined Tests and Three Phases), I began to train another young horse with more aptitude for jumping. I turned Farewell out to pasture for the winter with Fawn, a mare he had bred. When spring came, I pulled Fawn from the field so she could foal in the barn.

Farewell began pacing, and pacing and pacing. In his paddock he wore a rut as deep as his knees. In the barn he weaved. He stopped eating and lost so much weight that I could put a hand between every rib. My once chunky pony was unhappy; he was obsessed with the herd. I made the decision to geld him so that I could turn him out with the other horses.

At 11 years of age, he became the best-trained lesson horse in the barn. In a month, he was fat and happy to be finally out with his buddies.

Chapter 2

Knipper and the Cowboy

The lanky cowboy took his time exiting his pickup truck. Once standing, the sandy-haired man smiled broadly.

"Howdy, ma'am," he said as he tipped his Stetson hat. His voice was soft and low. "My name is Luke. I had called about taking a few riding lessons."

He looked to be in his early thirties. Despite Luke's pleasant demeanor and firm handshake, there seemed to be something odd about him. I was glad my black Labrador retriever sat next to me as I introduced myself and asked him about his prior experience.

"My uncle had a ranch in Texas when I was a boy, and I rode there most summers. I miss horses, and would like to get back in the saddle again, as the song says."

"So you want to go on a trail ride?"

I had just opened Unicorn Stables in Langhorne, Pennsylvania and had advertised private lessons and trail rides. My riding program included three horses and a pony.

"Well, ma'am," said the cowboy shyly as he fingered his silver, ornate belt buckle that he probably won at a horse show. "If you don't mind, I'd like a lesson in the ring. You do offer that don't you?"

I nodded, wondering why an experienced rider would want to stay in the ring. It was a lovely spring morning and this was no city slicker. Luke answered my unspoken question with his eyes looking down at his shiny leather cowboy boots.

"I just bought these boots. They were custom made for my new feet."

New feet? I was lost, and he smiled at my confused expression.

"Sorry, ma'am," he explained quickly. "I left rehab less than a year ago. I lost both legs in a minefield in Viet Nam. These are wooden."

He knocked twice for emphasis against his jeans. Sure enough, they sounded as hard as an oak table. Now I knew why it took him so long to get out of his truck. Then I thought, he drove the truck?

Luke followed my gaze to his old Ford.

"The brake and gas are rigged on the dash by the steering wheel. My left hand steers and my right gives me speed or brakes. A mechanic buddy fixed it up for me. Now I can get around by myself. My goal is to be able to do everything I did before the war. Riding a horse is at the top of my list."

"Oh," I said stunned. "Okay. I'm game if you are. Do you think you'll be able to mount by yourself, with just my help? There's no one else here but me." I was no longer worried about the strange cowboy.

"Do you have a mounting block?"

"Yes, so you can walk up steps?"

The question sounded dumb once I said it aloud. After all, he drove his truck.

"Slowly, I can lift these heavy legs. I use my hands under my knees. Do you have a horse quiet enough to stand still while I take my time to mount?"

"Yes, my horses fall asleep whenever they can during the lessons. Standing still won't be a problem. But with your height and weight, you'll need a big horse."

The cowboy may have looked slender, but with his heavy legs and muscled arms his weight would be too much for my small mare, Fawn. I had two geldings that stood over

15 hands, but one was young and although obedient, I wasn't sure what he would do if a wooden leg hit his side. Knipper won the coin toss.

The buckskin was a handsome fellow and very friendly. He also had a slow jog, if Luke ever progressed that far. Knipper was the type who would let a child ride him confidently walking like a turtle around the ring, and yet he could let loose at a full gallop with me down a dirt road.

I showed Luke the inside of the barn and watched him as he carefully placed each foot so he wouldn't trip in the dirt. Luke liked Knipper immediately as he patted the gelding's muscled neck. He helped me brush and tack up, and then we headed for the riding area.

I had set up a ring on the flattest section of the small farm, but it was at the top of a hill. I led Knipper as Luke made his way one step at a time. When I reached the center of the ring, Luke had only made it halfway up the incline.

"Do you need help?" I called down to him. Knipper ground tied if I had to leave him alone.

"No, I'm fine," said Luke in a labored breath. "Tighten his cinch and I'll be there in a minute."

I took the time to whisper to Knipper about the importance of his job today as I placed the mounting block next to the gelding's left side. I also lowered the stirrups on the big Western saddle all the way to the bottom. This is going to be an educational experience for all of us, I thought as I took a deep breath.

"Thanks, ma'am," said Luke panting as he stood beside Knipper. "I appreciate your patience."

"No problem, Luke. But please don't call me ma'am. Sharon will do fine. Now, what will be the best way for you to get on?"

By the trial and error method, Luke managed to heave his large body up on Knipper. It was a good thing the cowboy had strong arms. Sweat glistened on Luke's forehead as he sat tall in the saddle.

"There. Man, this feels so good!" Luke patted Knipper who, unlike my prediction, had stayed alert with his ears cocked back curiously, listening to what was going on. "Is Knipper voice trained?"

"Yes, but before you start moving, can I position your legs better?"

When he nodded, I pushed his leg under him and bent his mechanical ankle so that his heel was down. Then I switched sides and fixed his right leg.

"Does that make your upper body more balanced?"

"Yes, much better." Luke held the reins properly in his right hand and had his left hand rest on his thigh.

"I know you don't want to hold the horn, but promise me that if you feel like you're slipping sideways, you will grab it to save yourself. I'm not going to be able to run over and catch you if you start to fall."

He laughed. "I promise!"

Luke couldn't use his legs to kick, but with a firm voice he asked Knipper to walk. The buckskin obeyed, and true to form, Knipper walked sedately around the ring. Luke stopped him with his reins, seat and voice and then neck reined the responsive gelding the other way. I was never more than three steps away at first, but soon the pair walked confidently around the four barrels that made my ring. I stood in the center watching them. I was very impressed, with both the man and the horse.

After thirty minutes, Luke stopped Knipper in a square halt in front of me.

"That's enough for me today, Sharon. Would you please bring the mounting block over?"

I helped him as he swung his leg over and stepped gingerly on the top step. Luke almost fell backwards as the second boot landed but he grabbed the horn to balance himself. Knipper was a gentleman and stood as still as a statue.

I led the gelding back to the barn and Luke made his way cautiously to his truck. I untacked Knipper and turned him loose in the pasture with his stable buddies. I found Luke sitting sideways in his truck withdrawing money from his wallet.

"That's too much," I protested.

"Please take it. Riding again made it worth every penny. Buy Knipper a treat with the extra, okay?"

I smiled and took the cash. "You got your new boots dirty."

"Yeah, ain't life grand? See you next week, same time?"

"Sure, maybe you can try a jog. Knipper is real smooth and slow."

"Like a good cowboy song I bet," he said as he lifted his legs into the truck and shut the door. "So long!"

With a final wave, Luke backed down my driveway into the street. He paused as he pulled forward past the barn. I looked over into the pasture and there was Knipper rolling in the dirt. He flipped over to get the other side and then stood and shook off the dust, blowing his nose in contentment.

Yes, a good day was had by all.

Chapter 3

Grooming Clinic With Perlman

"Does anyone have any experience with horses?"

I stood in front of a group of girls visiting from a local summer camp. It did not have its own stable, but had requests for riding. So the director had asked me to teach the horse-crazy girls at my barn. The van had delivered the four 10 year-olds and their counselor for their first lesson. We had 45 minutes before they had to return to camp. The youngsters sat in front of me on bales of hay and as I spoke, I studied them. The girls varied in looks and sizes.

"I had a pony ride once when I was little," answered a petite, curly-headed blond.

"I fed a pony at the petting zoo a couple years ago," replied a long-legged, longhaired redhead.

"I brushed my neighbor's horse and fed it carrots last summer," said the skinny, braided brunette.

"And how about you," I asked the quiet girl with short hair and braces. "Have you ever been around horses?"

She shook her head slightly and I took that as a no.

"Your camp director said that you all love horses and want to learn," I added. "You'll be coming here three times a week for the next six weeks. You'll be learning how to ride and on the last visit, if I think you are ready, you'll go on a trail ride. Sound good?"

They all smiled and agreed. Even the shy one, who was chubbier than the other three, nodded willingly. Her name was Sara and she seemed scared but determined. I had the perfect horse for her size.

"First, you have to learn about horses from the ground before you get on them," I continued. "I'm going to explain the safety rules and how horses think, and then we'll have a grooming clinic. That means you'll be brushing, or cleaning, the horse to prepare it for the saddle. Okay?"

"You mean we won't be getting on a horse today?" Sara looked relieved.

"Not today. On your next visit, I'll have the horses tacked up and ready to go. You'll ride then. Today, you'll get to know your horse by brushing him. Any other questions before we start?"

The blond raised her hand. "Will we have the same horse every time?"

"Good question. For the first few lessons, yes, you will be assigned the same mount. Later, I may switch around. Horses are like people; they all have different personalities as well as looks. Each one can teach you something different."

I explained the safety rules to my attentive audience. Then I led four horses one at a time from their box stalls and hooked them on crossties set up in the aisle. A brightly colored Appaloosa stood in the front.

"This is a new horse, an Appaloosa, that just arrived yesterday. He's what some people call a loud Appy because of his many spots. A family whose children grew up and went off to college owned him. He's funny looking, isn't he? He's got a big head and big belly. He's overweight because he hasn't worked in a long time, but he's a real sweetheart and very gentle. There's just one problem. My friend who found him and brought him here didn't get his name. So you're going to name him, okay?"

The girls were immediately enthusiastic.

"How about we name him after our camp?" asked Sara while the others agreed.

"Camp Perlman? Yes, that suits him. Perlman it is. And because you named him, you can demonstrate how to brush him."

The chubby girl stood next to the chubby horse as I showed her how to use the grooming tools. Perlman wasn't very tall and didn't intimidate the youngster. Plus, he was dozing off while I spoke.

"While you brush him, you always want to keep an arm distance away from the horse," I explained to the campers. "Even though he is sleeping right now, he might stamp his feet at the flies. You don't want to get stepped on, and he won't know it's your foot. So keep your feet away from his."

"Horses sleep while standing up?" Sara was surprised.

"Yes, they can lock the joint at the top of their legs, called the stifle, and take a nap. See his head? It's level with his back, instead of up high, and his ears have flopped sideways. His eyes are half closed. Look at the back leg. See how it's bent? He's relaxing it while the other stifles are locked. It's just like when you wait in a line and rest your weight on one side."

I handed the grooming tools to Perlman's partner while the other girls watched.

"This round, black one is called the currycomb. You rub in circles on the fat part of his body, like you are erasing a chalkboard. Scrub hard to get all the dirt loose, but don't do his legs or face. When you finish this side with the currycomb, then you use the one with bristles, called the dandy brush, to smooth down the hair. Brush in the direction that the hair grows. You can use the dandy brush on the legs too."

Once Sara was currying Perlman confidently, I passed out grooming tools to the other girls and assigned them their horses. They enjoyed the chore as much as the horses enjoyed their massage.

When the campers were done with grooming the horses' bodies, I showed them how to feel with their palm to see if they missed any dirt.

"Sometimes you can't see the grunge, but you can feel it. It's important to have the saddle area clean, especially by the horse's elbow and belly where the girth will be tightened. If that area is dirty, the girth rubbing on it can cause an open sore. Then the horse can't be saddled again until it heals. Also, lift up the mane and feel if that area is smooth, and check the withers too."

After they made sure their horses were silky smooth, I showed them how to detangle the mane and tail.

"Spray a little Show Sheen first and then the comb can separate the coarse hair easier. Start at the bottom of the tail and work your way up. When you are done, you should be able to run your fingers through the mane and tail without feeling a knot."

Next, I demonstrated how to pick out the hooves.

"Always face the tail no matter what hoof you are picking up," I explained. "Run your hand down the leg and lean a little on his shoulder. When he rests his weight on his other legs and lifts his foot for you, be ready to catch it. Cradle it in your hand closest to the horse and hold it up as high as you can. If you hold it only part way, the horse will set it back down. Now, take the hoof pick and dig out the dirt in the hoof on the inside of the horseshoe. Look for the frog, which is shaped like the letter V. It is the tender part so be careful, but get out the dirt and stones in the ditches on each side of the frog."

Because the campers followed directions, the horses cooperated while all four of their hooves were picked out.

"Now you're going to paint their toenails!"

16

"Can we paint them pink like my nails?" asked the blonde as the others giggled.

"No, we brush on a brown-colored hoof dressing. It's like a moisturizer. Their hooves are similar to our fingernails but much larger. They grow about a quarter inch a month and the blacksmith will take off the shoe and file down the hoof about every six weeks. Then he'll nail on a new shoe."

"Doesn't that hurt the horse?" The redhead looked concerned.

"No, he feels a pounding but there are areas in the hoof that the nail can be hammered and it won't hurt him at all. The shoes protect the horse's soles from getting stone bruises."

I passed out cans of hoof dressing. The lids had built-in brushes and the students carefully painted the outer wall of the hooves while the horses dozed once more.

Then Sara called me over. She was doing so well I wondered what her problem could be and hoped Perlman hadn't stepped on her by accident. She whispered so that the others wouldn't hear.

"Just because Perlman is fat and funny-looking, he's a good boy, isn't he?"

"Yes," I whispered back, glad to hear the confidence in her voice. "He's a very good boy. In fact he's an angel."

The girl with braces smiled knowingly.

Chapter 4

Smiling on Dennis

After a decade of naming new horses, it was becoming a challenge to think of creative ones that matched. Often, we resorted to naming the horse after the person we got him from. Such was the case with the gelding that came from our blacksmith, Dennis.

Dennis, the horse, was a mixed breed with a copper colored coat and white blaze. His front legs toed in, and he was very stiff to move in a small circle. He wasn't very athletic, but he would work all day without complaint. And Dennis was reliable to stand rock-still and walk steadily.

When the director of the local Easter Seal Camp for handicapped children asked me about riding lessons, I knew I could count on Dennis to be in the group. The director wanted to bring out three children and she would provide the "walkers" who would stay on each side of the rider as they were led around the ring. The lessons would actually start out as pony rides until we assessed each rider for potential skill.

It was a varied group. One was blind and another had multiple sclerosis and used a metal walker. The third child was the one that stuck in my memory. He was autistic and his name was Brian. He was often lost in his own world.

The director had told me that all three children were between 10 and 12 years of age, and that they could follow simple directions. The youngsters had shown an interest in animals and the parents had agreed to the riding program.

The director was hopeful about Brian. She informed me that autism ranges from mild to severe, but that interaction with others can help improve the condition. Brian, diagnosed with mild autism, performed simple chores.

He willingly fed the cat, but he never showed signs of happiness. The director wanted to expose him to other animals to see if he would respond in a positive way.

Brian stared off in space as I explained the safety rules to the children and the helpers. A well-muscled counselor lifted each child carefully onto the saddle under my direction. I showed the helpers where to stand while my assistants led the horses. We started off very slowly, taking only a few steps and then stopping, before moving on again.

The blind girl loved to pet the horse's neck when we stopped, and then gleefully sniff her hand for the distinctive aroma. The young boy who couldn't walk without his braces and metal walker, sat tall in the saddle like a little cowboy, giggling as he rocked with the walk.

At first, Brian just sat hunched over on Dennis, with the walkers wary about letting him go. I couldn't tell if the boy was scared, but I decided to have them all come to the center of the ring for a game of Simon Says. Sometimes playing something familiar while on a horse will help a rider overcome their nervousness.

I had my assistants line up the horses in a circle around me, and told them we would play Simon Says on horseback. The director had told me that it was a favorite game at the camp and that the counselors even used it to encourage the children to clean their rooms or eat their dinners.

"Simon Says, touch your riding helmet," I instructed.

The helper gently guided Brian's hand to his head while the other two children touched their helmets eagerly.

"Good. Now, Simon Says touch your horse's mane."

My assistants showed them where the mane was located on the neck.

"Now, touch your horse's shoulder. Wait! Simon didn't say!"

The two children giggled while Brian gazed downward, frowning.

I had them pat the rump, shake the reins and touch the horn. Brian seemed to be sitting up a little better, so I instructed everyone to continue walking around the ring. This time I had the riders hold the reins and stop their horse.

Brian held the reins firmly and when I asked the group to halt, he actually pulled back and then rested his hand back on the saddle. Dennis stopped on command.

The adults and I were stunned. The youngster had not only listened to my instructions but also understood them. I asked the riders to walk on and about halfway around the ring said, "Simon Says, stop." All three children pulled back and relaxed, with the horses obeying easily.

"Perfect!"

What happened next, shocked us even more. It brought the counselors to tears.

Brian smiled.

In fact, he beamed. The corners of his usually drooping mouth curved upwards, forming dimples in his chubby cheeks. Brian's eyes gazed down at Dennis and he placed his other hand on the gelding's soft neck. Not a word was said by the boy, but no words were needed.

Welcome, Brian, to the world of horses.

Chapter 5

Flying on Sandy Mae

We had just moved to Honesdale when a mother set up an appointment for a private riding lesson for her young daughter.

"Hayley has had riding lessons for about a year, but all she has done is walk and trot," the mother explained. "I feel she is ready to move on, but her riding instructor says that Hayley would not be able to handle her horses at a canter. Can you teach her?"

As I listened to the concerned mom, I watched her six-year-old daughter play with the barn kittens in the hay. Hayley was an obvious animal lover.

"Was she taking English or Western riding lessons?"

"English, and she does know how to post the trot."

"Good. And she uses two hands to steer?"

"Yes."

"Has she ever ridden with her arms extended, without reins, to practice balance?"

"I'm not sure." The mother walked over to her daughter. "Hayley, did you ever ride with your arms out?"

Hayley looked confused.

"Did you ever ride without your hands on the reins," I added, "Like this." I held my arms straight out from my sides. "I call it airplane, like you are flying."

"Oh, yeah. When I first began lessons and I was still on the long rope," the youngster replied as she stroked a kitten's soft belly.

"She was on a lunge line for six months," explained her mother.

"That's fine. I'll have Haley ride Western today to evaluate her balance," I continued. "The Western saddle keeps her centered better, especially when she goes faster. Once I see how she posts the trot, then she can try the canter. Later, Haley can switch back to English. Okay?"

"You mean I can learn to canter today?" Haley left the kitten and stood to join her mother.

"If I think you are ready, yes, you can try it. You'll be on Sandy Mae. She's the best horse to teach the canter because her gait is slow. Sandy is a Welsh pony who's been teaching children all her life. Before we get started, do you have a helmet?"

"Yes, but she didn't bring her breeches and paddock boots," commented her mother. "Will her jeans and hiking boots be sufficient?"

"That's what most of my riders wear," I assured her.

The little blond girl dashed back to her car to retrieve her riding helmet. Before mounting the palomino mare, Hayley learned my barn and safety rules. Then, I explained that sitting in a Western saddle was the same as an English one.

"Usually your stirrups would be longer because you would sit the trot, but since you'll be posting, you'll have them shorter. Sandy has a snaffle bit in her mouth and today you'll learn one hand, the Western way. If you need to hold on for balance, hold the rim on the back of the saddle with your extra hand. If you're okay, then leave your other hand on your leg. That's right."

I had the pair walk around the ring, halt, turn around and walk the other way. Haley practiced circling a barrel to get used to reining with one hand. Sandy responded obediently to every cue.

Sandy stood 14-hands tall and was a chocolate palomino. She was dark tan in the summer and her winter coat came in a pale blonde coloring. She moved out nicely for an advanced young rider due to her background as a show pony when she was younger. Sandy could jump a two-foot course gracefully, and yet if a small child was just learning cross rails, she would trot slowly and smoothly while the young rider practiced balancing in the jump seat. Sandy's patience must have been developed during her time as a therapeutic horse in a handicapped-riding program before she came to camp.

Hayley proved to be an excellent student and quite talented for her age. She not only knew how to post the trot, but also knew her diagonals – rising up with Sandy's outside shoulder. With her confidence and balance, I felt she was definitely ready to move on. I shared my opinion with her mother who stood by the gate watching proudly.

"Hayley, come in the middle so I can explain the canter," I said. "Walking is four beats – all four hooves hit the ground separately. How many beats do you think the trot has?"

Hayley thought about it for a few seconds. "One?"

"Sandy would be hopping like a bunny if she only had one beat!"

Hayley giggled.

"There are two beats at a trot, Hayley, that's why you go up and down."

"I get it," Hayley smiled as she demonstrated her posting at a standstill.

"Now, at a canter there are three beats, so you won't be posting. You'll be sitting, like at a walk, but it will be much faster than the trot. Pretend you're in a rocking chair and rock your hips. Go with Sandy's motion because she is your dance partner, okay?"

"Okay, but how do I tell her to canter?"

"When I say 'canter,' you just tap her with your outside foot. She'll probably start when she hears me since she is voiced trained. Walk from this corner to the next. After you get there, ask her to trot, but do a sitting trot, and hold onto the back of the saddle with your extra hand. When you get to the next corner, I will say 'canter,' and you can tap her with your right heel if you need to."

"How will I know if she is cantering?"

"Oh, you'll know," I reassured her. "It's faster and smoother, and I'll say 'canter' again if she doesn't go the first try, okay?"

"Okay."

"Are you ready? Make sure your reins are down on her neck or she'll think you want to just trot. Hold onto the back of the saddle until your next turn."

Hayley guided Sandy along the side of the ring away from me. When she reached the top, she was sitting the trot as directed. As the pair began to head back, I shouted 'canter' loudly and Sandy responded willingly. Since she was accustom to this routine, Sandy stopped when she reached me. I gave her a well-deserved pat on the neck as I looked up to my smiling student.

"Great job, Hayley! Do you want to go again?"

Of course she did, and her balance improved with each effort. Soon, she didn't need to hold the back of the saddle. She rocked with Sandy's slow canter and kept her hands and legs in the correct position.

"Hayley, I think you're ready to try two-handed airplane while you canter. That's the test to see if you can switch back to English, because you need two hands for the reins. Do you want to try?"

Hayley was eager and I showed her how to drop the reins over the horn of the saddle to keep them out of the way when she let go.

"Same as before, Hayley, but when I say 'canter' you rock with her, but with your arms out to the side. Ready?"

"Yes! Let's go!"

Hayley guided the palomino mare around the ring as instructed, and at my command, the pair cantered in unison down the long side. The little girl's arms were outstretched and she shouted exuberantly as she came toward me.

"Look, Mom! I'm flying!"

Chapter 6

Chance Saves the Day

He was the most pitiful horse we had ever seen. The old gelding was a bag of bones, large bones of draft horse breeding, and full of bumps and open wounds. His neck was long, his tail short, and his spine was swayback. His color looked like it might be chestnut with a flaxen mane and tail, but it was hard to tell with all the mud and burrs. On a positive side, he had large, kind eyes and healthy hooves.

It was early spring and my husband and I were at our long-time friend's farm looking at his horses for sale. Earl was a horse dealer who knew the type of lesson horses I needed and had called me to see this gelding.

"I know he's not much to look at," Earl stated in his soft-spoken voice. "But all he needs is some TLC and groceries. Besides, any horse with a mustache is a good one."

Sure enough, there were long, soft hairs on his upper lip and jaw, making him look like a goat. Earl proceeded to tell us that he saved the old boy from the slaughterhouse. He was the right size and age, and possessed a quiet disposition for what I had requested – a mature, large horse to baby-sit timid riders on the trail.

So we took him home. I didn't even bother to ride him first since I felt he needed some meat on those bones before he should carry weight.

"Let's call him Chance," my husband said. "Because we're taking a chance on him."

I de-wormed him, gave him vaccines, had his teeth filed down – called floating – and increased his feed ration over a two-week period. Chance's appetite was good and after a bubble bath when the weather warmed, he actually started to look handsome in an odd sort of way. His red chestnut hair shined and his blond locks were tangle free. But it didn't matter about his looks anyway. My riding students adored him from the first day he arrived.

Lightweight, beginner riders learned on Chance until he was in good flesh and able to hold heavier riders. He was steady and reliable both in the ring and on the short trail around our farm. My students quibbled over who would get to ride Chance. They loved to braid his long mane and feed him apples or carrots.

We often had college students come for trail rides and sometimes a stocky athlete would bring his petite girlfriend. Invariably, after I evaluated the couple, it was the athlete I would put on Chance.

One early fall day, I took out such a couple on a longer trail through the state forest. They had ridden with me a few times previously, so I thought they might enjoy a change of scenery and the autumn colors. They were excited about riding for a couple of hours.

All went well for the first part of the ride, but on the way home we met face-to-face with a mangy, wolf-like dog. It bared its teeth and gave a threatening growl before attacking my horse. I was on a young Appaloosa I was training, and up to that point he had been as solid as a rock. But when the grey monster began biting at his legs, he reacted instinctively – he bolted. As I galloped down the dirt road, fighting for control, I could hear the dog barking at the other two horses. Bloody visions of my horses and riders flashed in my mind.

Finally, I was able to calm my distressed mount enough to slow him down and turn around. That was when I heard a yelp, and then all was quiet.

I jogged my sweaty Appaloosa back to my riders, praying no one was seriously injured. I found the couple laughing!

"Good boy, Chance," said the young man as he stroked the gelding's neck.

"What happened?" I asked in disbelief.

"Chance saved the day!" exclaimed the girl. "The dog tried to attack him and Chance kicked. He sent the mutt flying!"

"I've never seen a horse look so mean," added the guy as he continued patting Chance's shoulder. "He pinned his ears and kicked out with two hind legs. I almost fell off. I never knew a horse could be that powerful! His aim was so accurate that it just took one kick and he hit his target."

"After that dog landed, he bolted away on three legs," the girl continued. "I don't think you'll have to worry about him bothering your horses again!"

Chance had saved the day. I was sure glad we took a chance on him and brought him home.

Chapter 7

The Antics of Mini

Every morning the pony was out. Every morning I went to fetch her from the other side of the fence and return her to the pasture. But, every morning the pony was out. And the three-strand electric fence was never broken. How was she escaping?

Mini was a small, black pony with a long, thick mane and tail. She was very shaggy in the winter and from a distance she resembled a small bear. Mini was as gentle as a kitten but her escape antics were driving me crazy.

My husband and I had picked her up from our friend, Earl, a horse dealer. She was turned out in his hundred-acre field with other horses and he sent a young man out to catch her.

"You said you wanted a small pony for walk, trot lessons," Earl began. "One that didn't bite or kick. One that didn't spook."

"That's right. And this pony fits the bill?"

"Oh, she'll be quiet to teach with, but she does have one problem."

"What's that?" Every horse has a problem or two. It was a matter if I could live with it.

"She's hard to catch, see?"

Earl was pointing to his teenage worker, running after the pony trying to chase it toward us as we stood at the gate.

"She's never been in such a big pasture before. She's enjoying her freedom, I guess."

We laughed as the pony ducked away each time the poor guy tried to grab her halter. Earl looked relieved that I wasn't upset. He told the boy to chase her into the shelter next to the gate. Earl took a few ears of corn off a wagon and tossed them in the shed. With that enticement and the boy chasing her, the pony willingly went into the enclosure. We all surrounded her as she munched on the corn and she submitted to her capture without further fuss.

Earl hooked a lead rope to the pony's halter and instructed the skinny teen to ride her around us in a wide circle. The boy had to hold his legs up to avoid his boots from dragging on the ground. Despite the weird cargo on her back, the pony walked, trotted and stopped obediently with just the halter and lead rope. Then, as Earl explained more about her past life with a private family, the boy slid off her rear end and grabbed her tail and pulled. Then he got down on his hands and knees and crawled under her belly. The pony never flinched.

We took her home, satisfied that I could break that bad habit of not wanting to be caught. That evening, I fed her a handful of grain and left her in a stall with hay and water. I named her Mini. The next morning, after bringing in and feeding the other horses, I turned her out with the herd. They all greeted Mini as horses do, but she seemed content to graze by herself. I didn't have a hundred acres and the pasture was not as lush as Earl's field.

That afternoon, I called the horses to come in to eat, and they all came in as usual, except for Mini. She stood in the distance, watching. I left her there. She was fat and would survive missing a meal or two. I knew that when she became hungry, she would follow the others into the barn at feeding time.

And she did, eventually. The next morning it was the same routine except she stood closer to the barn door, watching. I talked to her as I cleaned and filled the water tub, but I didn't try to catch her. I turned out the well-fed horses and Mini seemed to understand what she was missing.

During the afternoon feeding, she walked into the barn after the others as if she had been doing it all her life. Mini let me take her by her halter and lead her into her assigned stall. She ate the small amount of grain greedily. When I turned her out, she blew her nose in contentment. She was home.

Mini proved to be the perfect lesson pony for small children. She didn't neck rein but she followed the line of horses along the rail quite nicely. She went to summer camp where the girls all rode English and, fortunately, I found a tiny English saddle and girth to fit her.

By the middle of summer, all the small girls wanted to ride Mini bareback. She was roly-poly and comfortable. She was a favorite for the short, slow trail ride around camp. I never had a small pony that could be trusted to go on a trail, but Mini enjoyed the walk through the woods on a hot day as much as the girls.

As the summer went on, the girls got braver. They wanted to try Mini at a canter. These girls were small and thin, but rode fancy show ponies at home. They wanted a challenge; one that was different from how high they could jump, or if they could make the horse swap leads on command. They did enough of that at home. They wanted to "train" Mini. We would see who was doing the training.

So I set up a time for a "Training Mini" session. The first few girls all were able to trot her bareback around the ring, but as soon as they asked for a canter, she resisted. Mini would stop suddenly and put her head down and to the inside. With no protruding withers to stop the rider, down the girl went, tumbling over Mini's thick neck.

An older, and heavier, girl was watching. She asked if she could try, so I let her mount. She was so tall that she simply swing her right leg over while her left foot was still touching the ground. She gathered up her reins and asked the pony to move forward. Mini took a few steps and stopped.

When the older girl asked her to move on, Mini's rump went up, not like a real buck, but definitely letting us know she would not tolerate this heavy rider.

The younger girls all had a good laugh, but the older rider suggested coaching them since she once had a pony at home that would also stop and put its head down. After many times hitting the hard ground, she had figured out how to ride that pony at a canter.

So she showed the most experienced younger rider how to shorten the outside rein to keep Mini's head up and facing toward the rail. She had the youngster grab a fistful of mane with her inside hand. I agreed that should work, and sure enough, Mini couldn't drop her head. It was a pretty picture to see the little black pony canter down the side with the camper smiling all the way.

The girls were not finished with their challenges to Mini. They taught her a trick. For food, Mini would do almost anything. They managed to have her jump up and place two front hooves on a small table, and then bow her head between her knees as if praying. She was actually looking for the carrot between her legs. Mini learned quickly and when she mastered the trick, the girls wanted to show her off to the rest of camp at the Talent Contest during the last week of the season.

Before the designated night, I had them practice taking her through the auditorium's back door, up two steps and onto the stage. I wanted to make sure that she wasn't too heavy and put a hoof through the floor. The wood creaked, but not even a hoof print was left.

For the big night, the girls braided Mini's locks and attached green and gold pom-poms, the colors of the camp. She looked darling, and the audience thought so too. When the curtain was opened, the crowd screamed and took photos. I held my breath hoping Mini wouldn't be frightened of the noise and flashing lights, and jump off stage onto the 400 people in the audience.

She loved it. When the audience settled down, one girl trainer on the microphone made introductions, and the handler then cued Mini for her trick. She performed like a true champ, and after a few times jumping up on the table and praying, I motioned the girls to get Mini off stage and out the back door before she left a wet present.

The following summer, on the first day the campers arrived, several new girls who had heard about our trick pony asked if they could sign up for Mini's training sessions. She was a hit every year she attended camp.

I did, finally, find out how Mini was sneaking out of the electric fence without breaking the wires. She had begun the ritual late in the fall, after her first year at camp. The pasture was dried up but the grass on the other side of the fence was tall and green. It was very tempting to a pony that had worked hard all summer.

One morning, a cold snap had left a light dusting of snow. I smiled as I approached the pasture and spotted Mini on the other side as usual. This time I was able to follow her tiny hoof prints and locate her escape route. There was a dip in the ground along the fence that I hadn't seen due to the tall grass. Mini had found it, probably by accident the first time, and was able to maneuver her pudgy but short body under the bottom wire, bending it but not breaking it.

After bringing her back to the barn and feeding all the horses, I went out and simply lowered the porcelain knob nailed to the post that held the wire. Mini would have to be able to crawl under eight inches to escape. She never did again.

Chapter 8

Floating on Flash

"What are the three type of trots?"

I stood in my ring surrounded by four intermediate riding students after they had warmed up their horses at a walk.

"A slow, medium and fast trot?"

Melissa, the teenage girl on Flash, was not shy to guess.

"You've got the right idea. The slow trot is called the jog in Western riding. In English, it's called the collected sitting trot. The medium trot is the working trot, and the fast trot is the extended trot. You can see and feel the difference by the way the horse tracks up. Let's start with the walk. The three speeds are collected, working and free walk. Do you remember what tracking up is?"

"When the horse's back feet step into the hoof prints of the front," answered Melissa.

"Very good. Can you walk Flash on the rail so the others can watch his stride?"

Flash was a 16-hand Thoroughbred cross. The middle-aged palomino gelding was as gentle as a mother with her newborn baby when he carried young children. Yet when asked to perform more athletic maneuvers, Flash's long legs and muscled body responded willingly.

"Melissa, how do you ask for a collected walk?"

"Shorten the reins and use alternating leg squeezes."

"Exactly. Go ahead."

The student, who was always serious about her riding, collected her reins slowly asking Flash to accept the bit and drop his head. At the same time Melissa alternated squeezing her heels against the gelding's belly to push him forward into her hands. By pressing the belly in the same direction as it swung, she was asking the back legs to stretch forward.

"It's like a Slinky," I explained to the other three students watching. "Right now, Melissa is pushing him together in a round frame, like pushing a Slinky closed. Watch his hooves. Flash's back feet are stepping into the tracks made by his front. His forehead is perpendicular to the ground, his neck is arched and his back is round while he uses his hindquarters to push forward. Okay, Melissa, demonstrate the working walk."

As the rider relaxed the reins a little longer, the horse's nose came forward.

"See how Flash's hind feet are over-tracking the front? It's like he's marching. Now Melissa, ask for a free walk. Relax the reins even more, but don't let him slow down."

The horse lowered his head reaching for the bit. At the same time, his rear hooves were over-tracking the front hoof prints by six inches. Flash blew is nose in contentment at being allowed to stretch.

"That's great, Melissa. He's over-tracking by a whole hoof print, like a Slinky pulled apart."

"I can feel it! He's really rocking his hips!"

I smiled as I waved to my demonstrator to join us in the center of the ring.

"The trot will be similar, but the aids will be slightly different. At the slow trot you will collect the reins and sit without posting. At the working trot, relax the reins and rise up as usual to the outside diagonal. When I ask for the extended trot, can anyone guess how to make the horse stretch his stride?"

The girls all looked at each other and then the three looked at Melissa.

"Relax the reins more and kick with your heels?"

"You are correct about the hand aid, but instead of using your legs, you will use your seat to push the horse forward. Just rise up higher as you post. Pretend you are on a bike and pedaling up a hill. You have to stand up and pump, right? Pump your horse by posting higher. Ready?"

The four girls guided their mounts to the rail in separate locations as they had been taught. My school horses played follow the leader for beginner riders, but for more advanced work, I wanted the horses' attention on their riders not each other.

"Let's practice the three walks first," I called.

They all followed my commands as they collected and stretched out their horses.

"Okay. That was great. Now, let's try the three trots. Start with posting the working trot to warm up. Get them settled into a steady rhythm."

Once they all found their correct diagonal and established a marching gait, I asked them for a slower, collected sitting trot.

"Stop posting, shorten your reins, but don't let them walk!"

Only one horse broke to the slower gait, and I took that opportunity to ask them a question.

"Halt please. Does anyone know the difference between breaking and a transition?

"Breaking is when the horse changes his gait when he hasn't been asked. A transition is when the rider cues the horse to change his speed to a slower or faster gait."

"Thank you, Melissa. Sometimes a horse breaks the gait because he thinks you asked him, so when you prepare for the sitting trot and collect the reins, use your seat and leg aids to keep him forward."

For the next fifteen minutes the riders practiced the sitting and posting trots. When they were ready, I asked for an extended trot.

"Loosen their reins slightly so they can stretch their neck. Now post higher. Pump!"

The girls tried but the horses didn't really over-track as much as they could have, so I called them into the center.

"To help the horse extend the trot you're going to use the cavalletti poles. Trot over them as usual but instead of balancing in your jump seat, I want you to post the trot while you go over them."

I had six white poles on the ground on the long side of the ring. Each rider took turns trotting around the ring and then over the poles, posting as the horse placed a separate hoof between poles. The horses' picked up their feet higher to clear the four-inch obstacle. The riders, who were accustomed to balancing in their jump seat, took a couple turns each in order to become comfortable with the bouncier posting trot. Then I lengthened the distance between the poles by a few inches.

"You still want only one hoof in each space, so ask for an extended trot on the approach to the obstacle. Loosen the reins and post higher. This exercise will help the horse to stretch."

After a few stumbles at the first attempts, the horses woke up and spread their stride correctly. I moved the poles a couple more inches apart and asked Melissa to go first.

"Remember to warm up first by asking for the extended trot before you get to the cavallettis."

What a sight the pair made as they glided over the poles. Flash's head was down as if sizing up the distance and his long legs stretched perfectly, elevating his body.

"Wow!" Melissa was excited. "That was awesome. I felt like we were floating on air!"

"Exactly."

Chapter 9

Montana and the Beach Ride

"Can I go with my daughter on the beach ride?"

Katie's mom, a petite woman in her thirties raising her teenager alone, had always helped around the barn, but had never ridden.

"Linda, the horses act very differently at the beach. Even if they are quiet and calm at home, they get excited when they see the ocean and ride in the sand. We won't be just walking, in fact, you can't hold them back from galloping."

"I'd really like to do this with Katie, since she asked me. What if I took lessons beforehand? We have three weeks, right? I could come in the mornings a few days a week while Katie is in school."

Yes, giving Linda private lessons might work. She was not a timid person and handled the horses on the ground just fine.

"Okay, but only if you let me be the one to decide if you're ready for the beach when the time comes."

"Great! I'll pay for as many lessons as it takes. Can I start tomorrow morning?"

I loved her enthusiasm. I decided to have her ride Montana, a Quarter Horse gelding that was broad but only stood 14.2 hands. He was a dark chestnut color and had impeccable manners. Whenever he was ridden at the beach, he had never given the rider any trouble. Also, his gaits were smooth which would benefit a novice.

True to her word, Linda rode three or more times a week. I had her ride Western and she enjoyed getting to know Montana while grooming and saddling him. Once mounted, she was nervous at first, but during the next several lessons she progressed from the trot to the canter. I had her practice the jump seat while trotting over ground poles and she even trotted over a small cross rail. When she was balanced and in control, I took her out on a short trail ride. The pair looked great together. Linda was a confident rider, with nice form and control, so I pronounced her ready for the beach ride.

Since we lived less than an hour away from the Atlantic Ocean, I would organize beach rides twice a year; in early May and again after Labor Day in September, when the crowds dwindled. We would park at Indian River Inlet on the Delaware coast. Horses could be ridden wherever four-wheel drive vehicles were allowed. The only people we usually saw were die-hard surf fishermen. It was easier to gallop on the sand when there weren't people sunbathing on blankets.

When you take your horse to the beach you have to understand how the horse thinks. Unlike common belief, all horses won't swim in the ocean. If you face your mount directly at the water, he sees the vastness and thinks you want him to cross it, so he balks at the first wave. Next, you try to walk him parallel to the water hoping to side pass him slowly into the ocean. But, the moving water creates an optical illusion and often when the waves crash against his knees, the animal sidesteps back out of what he perceives as a threat. In the twenty years we rode on the Delaware beach, only one horse, Fawn, made it past the breakers and swam over her head. But that's another story.

I usually took six horses in our stock trailer with ten riders. Everyone would help with grooming and tacking up the horses that were tied outside the trailer. I always rode bareback and a few experienced students who had practiced at home also chose to ride without a saddle. Some tacked up English while others, like Linda, rode Western. Fly spray and sunscreen were applied to both horses and humans.

I headed south on the sand with the first riders while the remainder of the group spread their blankets and ate lunch. After about an hour, we returned and switched riders. This time we rode northwards.

Linda and her daughter, Katie, rode in the second group. Linda confidently mounted and I could tell by her daughter's expression that the teen was proud of her mom.

"We're going to walk along the packed sand first," I explained to the five riders. "The horses will be more animated than when you ride them at home, but remind them you are the boss. And this is one place that we don't have to ride single file. The horses will want to band together as a herd against the unknown elements, so they won't try to fight each other. But, when we start to move faster, they will get competitive. They won't stay in a trot or canter for long. They will instinctively gallop in the sand."

"You mean they will run away with us and that's okay?" One of the college girls seemed concerned.

"What are they going to do? Run away to New York?"

That brought a laugh, soothing their nerves.

"Let them go," I continued. "And when I feel my horse laboring his breath, I'll be able to slow down, and so will all of you. Remember, the sand makes them work harder so they will tire sooner."

I explained the position for the gallop – rise up in the jump seat and hang on! And off we went, galloping side by side, with the horses in the firmer sand taking the lead. As I predicted, we hadn't gone far when the heaving horses slowed their pace willingly. We walked again to give them a break and passed some fishermen who whipped their lines out to sea. When the stretch of beach was clear, we took off once more. On our way back we repeated the procedure.

Linda and her daughter were doing very well. Linda held the horn and balanced in her jump seat during the first gallop. At the walk afterwards, her expression was happy, not scared to death, and she gave me a huge smile and thumbs up sign. Katie, riding English on a buddy of Montana's, proudly walked beside her mother, and at the gallop kept glancing at Linda to make sure she was okay.

In between runs, we attempted to wade in the ocean, but our coaxing was futile. Some of the horses, like Montana, had been to the beach several times. It didn't matter; there was no way they were going in past their knees and some wouldn't go into the water at all. But the group had fun at the attempt anyway. One rider, wearing shorts and a bikini top, dismounted and swam in to show the horses, but to no avail.

On the way back to our waiting group on the blankets, we got snagged – literally. We were walking side by side and had just begun to increase speed when one of the girls screamed. We all stopped and stared in disbelief. The rider, a young girl named Jessica, had been strangled by fishing line!

"The hook is caught on my horse's mane," said the college student. "But I don't see a fisherman nearby. Where did it come from?"

"We must have run into a line that was blowing in the wind," I guessed. "One end caught you and the other end somehow wrapped around Jessica."

Once we unraveled the line, a red mark was left on Jessica's neck, but she was laughing with the others at the strangeness of the incident. I was relieved that she was okay and after arriving back to our blankets, we had her hold ice from the coolers against her neck to prevent swelling. Many years later, Jessica's strangle marks faded but could still be seen.

We returned to the truck and trailer and loosened the saddles so we could walk the horses to cool them down.

"So, how did you like the ride?" I asked Linda who was walking Montana next to me.

"My legs are sore but it was exhilarating! On the first gallop I was a little nervous but Montana slowed down smoothly when I asked him. He really gave me confidence. Thank you so much for letting me ride with my daughter. This is something we'll never forget."

Chapter 10

April and the Prince

Summer day camp at Unicorn Stables was always a fun-filled week with a festive ending for the parents on Friday. The instructors and I would plan an activity to demonstrate to the parents what the children had learned. We would put on a skit, hold a small horse show or perform a drill team exhibition. But always there was music, and the riders and horses wore costumes.

In Honesdale, an old gray mare was added to our riding program. She had two sparkling blue eyes and the gentlest demeanor. I named her April since she had arrived during that month.

At summer camp, April was a favorite to the young or nervous riders. One session, a little boy was assigned to her, but he didn't look very happy on the first day. We were sitting on bales of hay in the barn discussing their goals for the week. There were five children, and Nicholas was the only boy attending with his two sisters. The other two riders were about the same age as his sisters, and the four girls made friends quickly. Nicholas sat on top of the highest bale of hay holding a kitten and keeping his distance from the others.

"So, what demonstration would you like to do for your parents on Friday? How about you perform a skit, or a short play, on horseback?"

"Can we do Snow White?" The oldest girl, who was Nicholas' sister, was excited. "I have a Snow White costume at home. I wore it last Halloween."

"That sounds like fun," I agreed. "Is everyone okay with that?" All the girls were enthusiastic, but Nicholas was silent as he stroked the kitten to sleep.

We went over our plans and I let Snow White choose roles for the skit – a wicked queen, two dwarves and a prince.

They chatted about their costumes while I climbed the hay and sat next to the young boy who looked like he didn't want to be there.

"We need a prince, Nicholas," I said. "I have the perfect horse for a prince. She's all white and she has blue eyes. Her name is April. Will you be the prince?"

"Is April real big?" He asked me in a whisper as he kept his blond head down and stroked the kitten.

"No, Nicholas. April is not real big. Actually she's a large pony. Why don't you come down with me and I'll introduce you?"

Nicholas gently set the sleeping kitten in a pile of hay and followed me to April's stall. I slid open her door and held her in the doorway. Then I saw Nicholas's face clearly.

"See, she has eyes as blue as yours!"

The youngster smiled for the first time and stroked the mare's neck. He appeared to be an animal lover, but wasn't happy about doing an activity with the girls. I hoped April would change his mind.

Snow White and the other girls joined Nicholas for their first riding lesson. All the children did rather well and even trotted in the Western saddles. Nicholas bonded with April and seemed a little more interested in the planned performance. After untacking and turning out the horses, he sat with the girls as they decided about the dialog for the play. With limited players and limited time, I told them to be creative and even make up their own story.

I was to be narrator, so the audience could follow the storyline. And what a story it became! It turned out more like a comedy. One of the parents even found a recording of the music from the play. They practiced all week and finally the big day came.

"Look what my mom made me!" Nicholas proudly donned a green felt vest and matching hat that would fit over his helmet. "See, it even has a feather!"

I was thrilled to see his enthusiasm for the event. "Yes, Nicholas. You look like a real prince."

The campers put the finishing touches on their horses and themselves. Snow White's costume made the girl look like she was headed for the ball, complete with flowers decorating her riding helmet. An artistic friend helped with the makeup. Soon they were ready for their families.

The drama unfolded with Snow White meeting the dwarves and learning to sing with them to the music.

"Hi Ho, Hi Ho, off to work we go!"

The children were comical as they trotted their horses around the ring. Then the evil queen cast her spell on Snow White and the young girl halted her horse and leaned backwards, resting her head on the horse's rump.

"Okay, Nicholas. Your turn," I said as I led him to the ring.

He walked April solemnly to the sleeping girl, and as he approached, he waved his wand and bonked her on the helmeted head.

"Arise fair maiden!"

The audience chuckled and then cheered as the riders marched and sang once again.

"Hi Ho, Hi Ho, off to work we go!"

Chapter 11

Jumping With Easter

"When can I start jumping like my sister?"

The twelve-year-old had started riding a year after her older sister, and had just learned to post the trot.

"Megan, we'll work on the jump seat over cavallettis today, and you can jump a cross rail when I think you are ready."

Megan was not the athlete that her sister was, but she had more determination and courage than most riders. I wanted to see her balanced while she trotted the poles without falling back into the seat.

I had been assigning her Easter because although he was tall at 16 hands, their personalities matched well. The chestnut gelding needed encouragement to move faster than a turtle, which became a nickname for him. Megan wasn't intimidated by his size and when he was sluggish she didn't hesitate to shout "trot" in a loud voice. Easter always woke up when Megan was aboard.

Easter's Return was a registered Quarter Horse. He knew his name, so when I began taking him to the Jewish camp, I didn't change it. I was sometimes questioned about it on Visiting Day but after I explained, the parents just laughed at the strangeness of it.

Visiting Day was always scheduled during mid-summer. It gave a chance for the campers to demonstrate to their parents what they had learned at camp so far. The beginners played games on horseback while I explained to the audience what the games taught the riders. The intermediate and advanced riders had a brief lesson to show how they had improved their trot, canter and jumping skills.

Megan's goal was to show off to her family by jumping on Visiting Day, just like her big sister.

The two siblings rode every day, although not always at the same time and never in the same class since they were at different skill levels. After a couple weeks of practicing the jump seat over the poles, I finally relented when Megan begged to jump a cross rail. I had the group line up at one end and set up cavalletti poles down the first long side and a very low cross rail halfway down the other.

"You will each trot around the ring one at a time, balancing in your jump seat over the poles. Post again until you reach the cross rail. Rise up as the horse trots over the jump and stay up until all four legs are past it.

"Okay, before we begin, let's review the five phases of jumping. Remember when you first learned them when going over the poles? This time, the obstacle will be higher and even though your horse will just trot and not actually jump over, he will pick up his feet higher. This will cause you to bounce and maybe lose your balance, so it's important to remain in the correct position and hold onto the mane. Who wants to tell me the first phase of jumping?"

"The approach."

Megan was not only enthusiastic about her riding, but also book smart. She absorbed information like a sponge, so I was not surprised that she knew the answer before the other girls.

"And what is important to remember about the approach?"

"It should be straight and forward."

"Exactly. Thank you, Megan. As you ride closer to the obstacle, make sure you are riding straight for the center of it and don't let the horse become too slow or he will stop before the jump. Or, he may go around it. Who's in charge of the approach, the horse or the rider?"

"The rider." All the girls responded together.

"Right. What's the next phase?"

"The take-off."

Megan and another camper said it at the same time and smiled at each other.

"And where is the take-off point? How far away from the obstacle?"

No one answered right away this time. Then Megan guessed.

"A couple of feet in front of the jump?"

"If it was a two foot jump, yes the take-off point would be two feet in front of it. But the cross rail is just twelve inches at the center. Where should the horse start to jump?"

"Twelve inches?"

"You're right, Megan. Good guess! And if it was a three foot obstacle?"

"Three feet in front of the jump."

"Yes, your memory is returning now, Megan. So what is the next phase?"

"The arc, or when the horse is over the middle of the jump."

"Good, and the next phase?"

"The landing."

"Exactly. Tell me, who is in charge of the take-off, arc and landing?"

"The horse." Megan beamed with confidence.

"Very good. That's why you rise up off their back and release the contact with their mouth when you are at the obstacle. The jump seat balances you in the center of their body as they pivot up and then down, like a seesaw. And you give them a long crest release with your reins, holding the mane at the same time, so that you don't pop the horse in its mouth if you lose your balance. What's the last phase?"

The girls were stumped once more.

"I'll give you a hint. It's what happens when you get better after being sick."

"Oh, I know now! The recovery!" Megan laughed with the other girls.

"Good girl. And who's in charge of the recovery?"

"The rider!" The campers all shouted in unison again.

"Yes, you must direct the horse and control the speed after the jump so you can be ready for the approach of the next fence. Today, the recovery will be to slow down to a walk after the jump, and then halt. Ready?"

"I am!"

Megan really wanted to go first, so I let her. She bobbled over the first jump but didn't let go of the mane and was able to straighten her seat on the recovery. Her tense expression changed back to her dimpled smile as she resumed her place in line.

"Nice try, Megan. Girls, keep your fist closed around the reins and mane just like Megan did to keep your balance. Make sure you feel your fingertips in the palm of your hand and keep your thumbs up, like you're holding an ice cream cone."

The girls practiced one at a time as I coached them from the center of the ring. I had to remind them to look up while jumping, as it's a bad habit to look down at the obstacle while going over it.

"Look up! Look up! Remember the horse is in charge of the jump. Let him look at it. You keep your head up and your heels down!"

During the next several lessons, Megan and the other girls improved their balance and I finally set up a twelve-inch vertical jump.

"Now the horse might actually hop over, maybe even canter over it. Approach it at a trot but when you get to the take-off point, let the horse decide how to get over. Balance with him until all four hooves are past it, and then sit back and slow him down. Ready?"

As usual, Megan wanted to go first and she balanced perfectly over the poles and continued to the vertical jump. Her approach was a nice steady trot, but she rose up into her jump seat too early. Easter took one stride at a canter and jumped the low vertical like it was twice the height. Upon landing, Megan lost her balance and fell over Easter's shoulder as he slowed down. She landed on her side but jumped right back up as I ran over to her.

"Well, that was lousy," announced the disappointed camper. "Can I try again?"

I made sure she was okay and then gave her a leg up. I coached the other girls over the jump, and they managed it just fine. That only made Megan more determined to do it right.

Her second attempt wasn't pretty either, but at least she didn't fall. By the third try, she began to get the hang of it. Even Easter acted like he was enjoying the lesson as he blew his nose during the recovery. Megan praised him verbally and with several pats on the neck.

Megan practiced her jump seat over cross rails and low verticals at the end of every lesson. She did improve each day, but she still lost her balance occasionally, sometimes hitting the dirt in the process. But her dimples always shined as she dusted herself off and remounted. The young girl realized that it wasn't Easter's fault when she lost her balance. He always stopped immediately after her fall and sometimes turned around to sniff her if she didn't stand up right away. That made the young girl feel better.

Visiting Day arrived and Megan was obviously nervous when she arrived at the designated time to show off for her parents. The riders were to give a 15-minute demonstration, and when Megan walked in the barn she looked toward the ring to see her favorite mount with another camper aboard.

"I'm riding Easter, right?"

"Yes," I assured her. "As soon as that rider dismounts, you can get on him and adjust your stirrups. We'll start the demonstration when you are ready."

I had the small group walk and trot around the ring both ways and then canter one time halfway around the ring before lining them up to start the jumping demo. I purposely set up the poles and jump exactly how we had been practicing in lessons. Horses and children are more comfortable with what they already know.

Megan was the last of her group to approach the poles and take the jump. She trotted over both obstacles like a pro. Her head was up and her heels were down, and she had Easter moving out in a lovely working trot. She nailed her take-off points and Easter responded with precision.

I raised the cross rail to a low vertical, just like in the lessons. When it was her turn, Megan steered Easter perfectly over the cavalletti poles in a lovely jump seat.

However, on the approach of the higher fence, her nervousness took over. I watched her close her eyes and hold her breath as she rose up in her jump seat three feet before the vertical. Easter responded by jumping early and long, and of course the young girl found herself in the dirt once more.

I thought she might be embarrassed if she fell in front of a crowd, but instead of crying, she stood with her arms out and said, "Ta da!" And then she bowed.

The audience's applause was so loud that the parents watching the gymnastic meet next door turned their heads to see what was going on in the riding program. I was standing next to Megan's family and explained what she did wrong. They didn't seem upset and probably had heard about the practice sessions in their daughter's letters home.

Megan remounted with an instructor's help and lined up to take the small course again. This time she balanced perfectly over both the poles and the jump, causing the audience to clap even louder.

Megan's rosy, dimpled cheeks gleamed in the sun as she leaned forward to kiss her buddy's neck.

Chapter 12

Sundance the Picnic Lover

Some horses are destined to be the center of attention, the comic among the serious, or the class clown. Sundance was such a horse. He was a muscular pinto that stood just over 15 hands. Sundance's looks – the handsome Quarter Horse build, dark eyes and long, bushy tail – belied his devilish personality.

None of his antics were meant to be deliberately mean or rude. He just wasn't shy about expressing his desires, which usually centered on food. Not only did he love grain, apples or other horse treats, but also human delicacies. Sundance loved a picnic.

As soon as the grill was fired up in our yard and smoke wafted across the pasture, Sundance trotted over to see what we were serving. He tested anything, including a hot dog, piece of watermelon or marshmallow. But a can of soda was his favorite. He could even hold the can in his large mouth while slurping the sweet treat.

One of his favorite activities was a picnic trail ride. I would escort a group of a dozen students on a long horseback ride to the Salisbury Zoo or county forest. When we arrived at our destination, we dismounted and unpacked our bagged lunches. If no bench or fallen log was available, we sat on rocks or the grass.

Sundance would start sniffing his rider's snack and invariably he would receive a piece of peanut butter and jelly sandwich. He wouldn't stop there. He'd moved to the next closest rider and begged for some bologna.

"I thought horses weren't carnivorous," said one teenage boy. "Can I feed him some of my bologna sandwich?"

"Give him only a very small piece," I replied. "He may spit it out."

Sundance devoured the treat and licked his lips after swallowing it. At least he never nipped at the human fingers. I always made sure the riders kept their palms flat and only gave small amounts. Surely, bologna could not be nutritionally good for a horse's diet.

Still curious, Sundance sidled over to the next mark where he tested tuna and potato chips. One rider offered grapes and pretzels. They were very much to his liking. The children laughed as they enjoyed the odd picnic partner. They even tried to offer their own horses a human treat, but the others dismissed the offerings preferring the grass instead. Not all equines have sophisticated tastes I guess.

Sundance never became sick from eating the human delicacies, although there were some items he found distasteful. He would curl his upper lip, showing his teeth and gums. One youngster at a horse show tried to feed him tortillas and salsa, and Sundance let us know he didn't care for the Mexican treat. Chinese food was also not to his liking, as he dropped an egg roll he was offered during day camp. A mother had delivered a hot lunch for her children and brought an extra egg roll for Sundance. Maybe it needed the sweet duck sauce.

Sundance's rider had to be wary when passing by a fruit and vegetable stand while on the trail. The greedy horse would sniff it and try to help himself to squash, apples or whatever was displayed. If he was successful, the rider had to pay for Sundance's selection.

Sundance's favorite place to eat was at BJ's Market, a small convenience store near our farm. After a long trail ride through the forest, we often stopped at BJ's on the way back for snacks and drinks. While eating French fries and guzzling soda, Sundance gained the attention of other customers. When the crowd became too large I said it was time to mount and head home. I always made sure my students wore their Unicorn Stable T-shirts. Invariably, shortly after our picnic rides, I would receive phone calls about riding lessons on the brown and white horse who liked to drink soda.

Yes, Sundance was my best form of advertisement.

Chapter 13

Magic Memories

"I've got the perfect horse for you, Sharon."

My husband and I were visiting Earl's auction barn and his adult son, Ronnie, flagged us down as we drove into the dirt driveway one October afternoon. We always arrived long before the auction started to view and ride the horses for sale. We often loaded a horse or two onto our trailer and left before the auction began as we had a long drive home and a horse show to attend the next morning. Earl and Ronnie knew what type of school horses I liked and would eagerly show them off so that I could have the first viewing.

After we parked, I found Ronnie leading a large gray pony in the driveway. She looked to be an Arabian cross with a slightly dished face and high tail set. I checked her teeth and legs as Ronnie explained that he took the mare in trade. The family wanted a larger horse for their daughter who was into the show scene and needed a 16 hand horse for the larger fences. This mare stood 14.2 hands at her withers.

"Does she jump?" I asked.

"She's suppose to be a willing jumper, but my boy hasn't tried her out yet," answered Ronnie. "Why don't you hop on and jog her down the drive while I rustle up a jump for you."

I liked her immediately as I rode her up and down the driveway bareback with just an English snaffle bit in her mouth. She was comfortable and obedient. More important, when I passed another horse being tried out, she never pinned her ears.

"Here, Sharon. Try her over this."

"You're kidding!"

Ronnie and his teenage son were each holding the end of a two by four. "Come on," he encouraged. "We'll hold it low to start."

I trotted the mare forward and she pricked her ears as we approached the odd jump, but she hopped over willingly. The guys held the board up higher, about two feet off the ground. I turned the mare and asked for her to take the higher obstacle. Again, smooth as silk, she took the fence like a pro, even blowing her nose in contentment afterwards.

"What's her name?" I asked Ronnie as we loaded her into our stock trailer.

"They called her Magic."

We took her home and the sweet mare adapted to our barn right away. Our son, Josh, was about 8 years old and wanted to learn how to ride English on Magic.

"You sit the same way, Josh," I explained during an after school lesson. "The English saddle is flatter and doesn't have a horn, but you have good balance and don't hold on anyway. You will still have an imaginary straight line from your shoulder, to your hip, to your heel."

Once he was mounted and I had adjusted his stirrups, I showed my young son how to hold the reins.

"Hold one rein in each hand, with your pinky closer to the horse's mouth," I said as I placed the reins in his small fists. "Keep your hand closed and thumb facing up, just like Western, but now you have both hands in front of you. Rest them on the saddle until you need to give Magic a signal, like stopping or turning. There should be another straight line from the horse's mouth, through your hands to your elbow. When you want to slow down or stop, you just need to squeeze your fists to put pressure on her mouth. See?"

I demonstrated by gently pressing on Josh's fists and as the reins became tighter, Magic dropped her head a little and took one step backwards. I relaxed the reins and the mare stopped.

"Because she was already stopped, Magic thought you wanted her to back up. Now, try squeezing just one fist."

Josh complied and the mare turned her head in that direction.

"That's how you steer, Josh. Your hands don't leave her withers. Just slide your hand down the reins if you need to shorten them, and then just squeeze while your hand is just above the saddle. Good, you've got the idea!"

Always an attentive student, Josh picked up the details of English quickly. For adults, I explain that the difference between the two disciplines is not only the looks of the saddle, but also the contact with the mouth. The Western horse is taught to be an independent thinker with no contact on the mouth except to slow down, stop or reverse. When he's given a command, he stays there until the next signal. A horse ridden English has every step controlled by the rider, with the only time there is no contact on the mouth is during a free walk where he can relax his head, or a long crest release given by a beginner rider during jumping.

For children as young as Josh, I leave the abstract thinking out of the lesson. Josh had learned how to post on a Western saddle so when he was ready to move on to the trot he remained balanced and in control.

"Can I canter and jump now?" Josh's enthusiasm was equal to my other students who progress as quickly. But this mom wasn't going to watch him try the more difficult maneuvers.

"Next lesson. Melanie can teach you."

My instructor took over Josh's lessons on Magic throughout the winter, and several months later she told me he was ready to enter in the spring horse show. We had planned a Combined Test and signed Josh up for the

Walk/Trot Division. He would ride a simple Dressage test and then jump a course of six cross rails.

Josh was excited as I dressed him in his navy jacket over a white shirt and tan jodhpurs. He slid on his shiny riding boots and pulled on his new riding gloves. I fastened his riding helmet snugly.

"When do I ride?"

"This morning you ride Magic in the Dressage test, the pattern you practiced with Melanie. Remember?"

"Yes, Mom. I know it. But when do I jump?"

"Not until after lunch. So when you finish the test, take off your jacket, helmet and gloves and put them somewhere safe so they don't get lost or dirty."

"Yes, Mom," he sighed.

He was a good boy that always listened to his mother. When he completed the Dressage test, successfully I might add, he removed those three items and found a safe place in the barn to store them until his afternoon jumping competition. They were the only things that remained clean.

When the stadium jumping started, Josh was nowhere to be found. He finally came running when he heard his name on the loudspeaker. His face and hands were dirty, as were his new riding pants and boots. There was no time for a complete wash up since he was the last rider entered in the cross rail division, and the fences needed to be raised. Using a paper towel I wiped his face and hands the best I could and he donned the rest of his outfit as we walked to the ring.

Melanie, finished with another student, came over to help. She laughed as she mounted him on Magic and adjusted his stirrups.

"At least they don't take off points for dirty faces in the stadium jumping!"

I smiled back and then looked at my son. "Josh, you go around the ring and take the four fences and then change rein and take two more. You got it?"

"Yes, Mom." He sounded confident as Melanie and I watched him enter the ring, halt squarely, and salute the judge.

"So, he knows all the rules of stadium jumping?" I asked and Melanie nodded.

I liked the Combined Tests because the jumping phase was easier than in an English Pleasure or Hunter show. The rider is allowed to walk or trot the course, or even do both. He can lose his balance over a jump but as long as he doesn't fall, no points will be deducted. But he must salute the judge upon entering the ring, wait for the signal to start, ride the course in the proper order with the red flags on the right, and pass through the finish line after the last fence.

I thought Josh began well even though I heard Melanie say, "Uh oh."

Six fences at a trot went quickly and he passed through the finish line with a smile. Josh halted in front of the judge who stood near the gate where Melanie and I waited.

"Nice job, young man," we heard her say. "Your position was great and you did very well, except you went the wrong way around the ring and jumped all the fences in the wrong direction. Know your course next time."

Well, at least jumping Magic at his first horse show gave him a thrill.

Chapter 14

Fievel's Costume Class

Halloween was always a favorite time for my riding students. I held a horse show just for them and we had a party afterwards. My son helped out with the festivities by building a Haunted Barn, or a maze in the hay. Josh and his school buddies began in September moving the bales and deciding what scary outfits they would wear.

The Costume Class was the high point of the horse show. Often, riding students would plan their costume months in advance. Prizes were awarded to every entry, with a special prize for the most original. The week before the show, I signed up my students for the classes they wanted to enter. The parents told them how many they could do, and I helped the youngsters to choose according to their skill level.

One year, we had a very creative mother design a costume that was quite remarkable.

"I need a white pony for the costume class," said Susie, a young beginner rider.

"What are you going to be?"

"It's a secret," she whispered.

"It's okay. I won't tell anyone else."

I was amused when I heard the description from her mother. It was a clever idea, and I picked Fievel to be Susie's partner, because if any horse could handle her costume, it would be the short, fat gelding with the bombproof disposition. And he may encounter bomb-like situations before the show was over.

My son had named Fievel after the mouse in the Disney movie. The 14-hand pony looked to be part Morgan with his large eyes and friendly attitude. He loved children but he tended to be quick so I only had more experienced riders on him during lessons. If he was led, however, he walked slow and steady and I often took him to pony parties if the children were older and too big for my small ponies. He was my favorite to ride as a lead horse, be it on a trail or at the beach. His chubbiness and smooth gaits made him very comfortable to ride bareback.

When I held horse shows for just my own students, I scheduled classes that were fun. The games the beginner children played on horseback were exciting as usual – Musical Chairs, Red Light Green Light, and Simon Says etc. The more advanced riders entered gymkhana games like Cloverleaf Barrels, In and Outs (Pole Bending around barrels), and Scurry Race (jumping over low fences while cantering around the ring.)

After the last game of the day, I announced that there would be a break so that the first group could dress up themselves and their horses for Costume Class. We had such a large number of entries that I split them into two groups of eight riders each.

When the contestants were ready, they marched into the ring. One little girl was dressed as a bride and her pony was the groom complete with a top hat and tie around his neck. We had the usual witch and vampire, and we even had a girl dressed as a racing jockey. Other children wore their Halloween costumes while sitting on a horse. Everyone received a bag of candy, and the bride won the ribbon for the most original.

Then the next set of riders entered. We had Raggedy Ann and Andy on matching ponies, a clown, a cowboy and a few other store-bought costumes.

The last to enter was Susie on Fievel, with her mother leading the pair. But you couldn't tell who the girl was because she was dressed as the California Raisin and the white pony was covered in purple balloons!

As Susie accepted her candy and ribbon for the most original, a balloon popped. Fievel lifted his head but never spooked.

They walked out of the ring slowly and Fievel blew his nose as if to say, "Thanks goodness that's over. Now get these weird things off me!"

Chapter 15

Leg Yielding With Tetris

Do you remember the video game named Tetris? When it first came on the market, I thought that the name was so cool that I would name a horse after it. But not just any horse, it had to be as cool as the name.

A Thoroughbred-cross mare was available from a friend who sold us a few horses over the years. He knew we needed a big English horse for Lake Bryn Mawr Camp. He brought a 16.2 hand mare from Virginia that had competed in three-phase events. Due to a serious injury to her shoulder, she had been out to pasture for a few years. She was now sound but with an obvious disfigurement in the form of a sunken pocket on her lower neck preventing her from ever showing again at the level she had competed.

I tried the bay mare out in the small grass yard and within two minutes knew I wanted to take her home. She responded easily to my leg pressures to leg yield at a walk, and when I asked her to accept the bit, she dropped her head and gave willingly. I trotted her in a collected frame and she was definitely sound. In fact, I would need to work her down a peg, as she was almost too eager for my campers, even the most advanced riders. I named her Tetris.

On the first day of camp just after settling into their cabins, the riders would flock to the barn to visit their favorite equine friends and see who was new. They were all impressed with the size of Tetris, for she was the tallest we ever had at camp. They loved her arched neck and large brown eyes. Everyone asked about her ugly scar but I assured them that it didn't hurt now.

The riding staff had ridden Tetris and the other advanced horses during the week before the campers arrived.

Only two others beside myself were able to keep Tetris in control. She was super sensitive. If the rider accidentally touched her sides with their heels, she would move sideways. If they squeezed too hard on her reins, she would move forward into a collected canter. Then, if the rider was not balanced, Tetris would become confused and gallop around the ring, causing the rider to fall. She was never mean, she just didn't understand what was being asked.

Yet, if you knew what buttons to push, Tetris was a dream to ride. She just had to become accustomed to many different partners aboard and I felt that after her first summer, she would relax and learn the program. I loved having horses with "higher education" in my program, but they had to learn to wait until the rider asked for upper level movements.

Lateral movements were Tetris' field of expertise. As a young rider mounted, often Tetris misunderstood when the small foot touched her side as a stirrup was being adjusted. Tetris would turn on the forehand thinking that's what was being asked. Then the child would wonder why she was going in circles.

Because of her sweet disposition, both on and off her, Tetris was never hated by the campers. In fact, she was often requested. The advanced riders would line up to ride her, and after a fall, I would say, "Next!"

I lunged Tetris at a walk and trot while the rider became settled to the mare's sensitive ways. But, after they were sent down the rail on their own, many riders became tense and sent mixed signals to Tetris. The sensitive mare responded immediately by increasing speed, causing the rider to lean forward and tighten the reins as she tried to hold on. Tetris would pick up more speed and the rider would hit the dirt when they turned a corner.

One young lady did extremely well. As soon as Amy mounted Tetris the first time, I knew they would work well together. She was an older camper who had ridden with me for several summers. Even though she never rode at home, she always looked great getting back on a horse, and increased her skills each year. She was one of the handful of older girls who had requested upper level horses. Tetris fit the bill.

"Let's take it easy the first few lessons," I explained to Amy on her first day riding. "When your legs get back in shape I'll show you all the moves that Tetris knows. How about you trot her around the ring without letting her break into a canter."

"I bet she can do a nice extended trot with her long legs," predicted Amy.

"Yes, she can. But let's try that later."

Amy had Tetris trotting steadily around the ring, and when I asked for the group to change rein at a trot, Amy was able to keep the mare under control. She had Tetris on the bit in a round frame, and changed diagonals exactly in the middle. When I asked the group to walk on a loose rein, Tetris dropped her head below her poll and blew her nose in utter contentment.

Amy had signed up to ride every day and she usually was assigned Tetris. After a few days, I had the pair canter around the ring and Amy kept Tetris collected. Soon they were performing a canter in a figure eight with a flying change of leads.

Jumping sessions started with cavalletti poles and Amy helped Tetris learn to relax as she trotted over them. Tetris loved to jump, but I needed her to learn to trot cross rails until she was asked to canter them. Amy spent all summer half-halting the big mare before the jump and praising her when the horse complied and trotted smoothly over the low jump.

Eventually, Amy and Tetris were cantering higher jumps and even jumping courses of six fences. To relieve the stress of ring work, Amy took Tetris on her first trail rides and convinced the mare to drop her head on a long rein and relax.

One day, at the end of summer, I spoke to Amy at breakfast.

"I think you are ready to try the lateral moves on Tetris."

"That would be great!"

When she arrived for her lesson, I had assigned just two other riders to be in her group, since there were only three horses at camp that knew how to perform turn on the forehand, the leg yield and the side pass.

"Line up your horse parallel to the rail," I instructed. "Halt square, please."

I showed them how to use their leg and hand aids to move the horse's rear end 180 degrees while pivoting the front end in the same spot.

"Make sure you keep the horse straight from the poll to the tail, and don't let him move forward. The back end does not have to move quickly. Take one step at a time."

They all tried the maneuver a few times, with Amy and Tetris doing it the best. I asked them to walk on the rail in a collected frame to prepare for the leg yield.

"While you have your horse's attention, squeeze gently with your outside rein until you can see the horse's outside eyelash and nostril. Now, gently push with your outside heel so the horse moves away from the rail. He should take one step forward and then one step sideways. Very good, Amy. When you push the correct buttons on Tetris, she responds immediately, doesn't she?"

"I can feel her crossing her legs!"

"Exactly. Now let's turn on the forehand and try the leg yield at a walk in the other direction."

When all the riders began to get the correct response, I asked them to sit the trot around the ring.

"When you leave the short side of the ring and begin down the long side, ask for the leg yield. You give the same aids as when you were walking but make sure they are doing a working trot. If they are too slow, they will probably break to a walk when asked to move sideways. If you have them too fast, they may break to a canter."

Sure enough, when Amy asked Tetris to leg yield, she had the mare trotting too strong and Tetris broke into a canter.

"Remember, when you use your outside rein and outside leg, those are the aids for a canter. Keep her steady with the inside rein and your seat. Good, Amy! You did it that time!"

After a few tries, I had them all walk to cool off the horses while I explained the side pass and set up poles.

"This time you will move your horse sideways without going forward. There is one cavalletti pole set up for each of you. Stop your horse on one end with the two front hooves on one side and the back hooves on the other. Now, using your leg and heel, press the side so he moves away from the pressure just like leg yielding. Use the same rein aids but prevent your horse from going forward and stepping over the pole."

Only Tetris was able to perform the difficult side stepping without assistance from me.

"This is one cool horse," stated Amy as she finished walking sideways over the pole.

"Yes, she is."

Chapter 16

Oakley Wins Musical Chairs

Sidney was a dark-haired, wide-eyed eight-year-old who loved to ride Oakley. Their quiet and gentle personalities matched well. When it was time to assign horses to my group of riding students, Sidney pleaded with those doe-like eyes but never said a word. When I told her she would ride Oakley, she would smile shyly. Before she began brushing Oakley, she would give the old mare a hug.

Oakley was a 14.2 hand bay pony with a wide blaze and front stockings. Due to Cushings Syndrome, her body hair was long, even in the summer. She would shed the thick winter coat in the spring as horses do, but she grew back more long hair because her pituitary gland was confused. It always took a little longer to brush her, but Sidney never minded. She would seriously rub the half-asleep mare with the currycomb to remove the dirt, and then gently stroke the dandy brush until Oakley's coat was silky soft. The mane and tail were thick and long much like Sidney's. One day, I showed the students how to brush the mane and tail.

"Use the Show Sheen to get the tangles out. Just spray it on and then it will comb out much easier. Start at the bottom and work your way up."

"Is it like when my mom puts cream rinse in my hair after the shampoo so she can comb it without hurting me?"

"Yes, except this doesn't have to be rinsed out. When we give Oakley a bath, we'll use cream rinse then."

"Can I help give Oakley her bath?" Sidney's eyes sparkled when I told her yes.

"We'll have a bubble bath party when it's warmer. I'll make sure your parents know so you can help."

Sidney reminded me every lesson until finally the day arrived. I planned a horse show for my local riding students prior to when the horses would go to camp, and the weekend before that was a good day to give all the horses baths. Sidney and three other enthusiastic students offered to help. None of the children had ever bathed an animal larger than a small dog.

"How do you fit a horse in a bathtub?" asked Sidney.

"Washing a horse is more like washing a car," I replied with a laugh. "We don't put the horse in the bubbles. Instead, we put the bubbles on the horse."

I squirted a little shampoo into a tall bucket and filled it with water. When the bubbles reached the top, I turned off the hose. I had Oakley and another pony outside on the grass. One child held the lead rope and the other would wash one side. Then they would switch.

"Dip your dandy brush into the bucket," I explained. "Scoop up some bubbles and put them on your horse. Swish the brush around so the soapy water reaches all the way to the skin under the hair. Keep dipping your brush to get more bubbles. Start on the neck, go down the back to the rump and then scrub the legs."

Sidney washed Oakley first as her partner held the grazing pony. As usual, the little girl was serious and gentle. She made sure bubbles didn't go into the old mare's eyes. When both ponies had their bodies wet and soapy, I showed the students how to rub some shampoo directly onto the mane.

"Wash the mane like you wash your hair. Get it nice and soapy. Next, we'll dip the tail into the remainder of the water in the bucket. Add some soap and scrub! Good. Now it's time to rinse."

It was a warm day, and the children had fun playing with the bubbles. They had lathered the horses, themselves and then flung some bubbles at each other. Holding the hose, I showed them how to rinse the horses.

"I'll hold the horse while you take turns rinsing the side you washed. Rinse the mane and neck first. Be careful not to splash the horse's face. We'll wash the face with a towel afterwards. Now, hose the body and use your hand to scrape away the bubbles. That's it."

Next, I poured cream rinse into their palms so they could rub it into the manes and tails. Taking the hose once more, the children did the final rinse.

Soon, both horses were wet and shiny. They continued grazing as I showed the children how to scrape off the extra water with the sweat scraper. Using large combs they detangled the manes and tails easily. I wiped each pony's face with a wet washcloth.

"There," announced Sidney when she and her partner were done. "Oakley is ready for the horse show. Isn't she pretty?"

"Yes, she is. And you both did a great job washing her."

The horse show was only for my riding students and included games. Some classes were timed with a stopwatch and others were won by process of elimination. Sidney signed up for three events, all on Oakley of course. Simon Says, Red Light-Green Light and Musical Chairs were designated for her beginner level.

Simon Says helps the riders remember the parts of the horse and tack. It also teaches them to listen and follow directions. The class begins with the riders on their mounts standing side-by-side in the center of the ring.

"Simon Says, touch the mane."

The six riders obeyed and I continued giving parts of the horse or equipment to touch or point to, such as the rump, the hoof, the withers, the bit and the stirrup. Sidney

85

got them all right, but one boy touched his helmet without the Simon Says command and he was eliminated. Another girl was out when they were asked to walk around the ring according to Simon Says, and then asked to halt without the Simon Says command, and she stopped.

Sidney walked and halted fine as she followed directions but was out when the riders were asked to trot and Sidney couldn't get Oakley to increase speed quickly enough. After several attempts, I had to announce that she was out. She smiled as she dismounted and led Oakley out of the ring.

When that class finished, Sidney joined four others in Red Light-Green Light. The riders lined up side by side at one end of the ring and the goal was to race to the other side. But they were only allowed to walk or trot when my back was turned and I said, "Green Light." When I turned to face them and said, "Red Light," the riders had to be at a halt. If more than three steps were taken at that time, they would have to return to the starting line. The game taught the riders to use their aids correctly in order to have the horses respond obediently.

Sidney had no trouble getting Oakley to halt quietly. But with her short legs, she couldn't get Oakley to trot quickly enough and the pair came in last place. Sidney continued to smile as she received her fifth place ribbon.

Then came Musical Chairs, and Sidney proudly walked her favorite horse around the ring while the music played. When the music stopped, the riders halted their horses, dismounted and ran for a crate to sit on while their mounts were left at the rail. At each pause, one rider was eliminated. One crate would then be removed and the riders would remount with assistance as needed. This game taught emergency dismounts in a safe way.

Sidney and Oakley did well. Oakley stopped easily and Sidney would kick off her stirrups and jump down faster than the other riders. She was always first to sit on a crate.

Soon, it was only Sidney and one other rider. I asked them to trot this time around as the music played. To Sidney's delight, Oakley followed the other horse into a trot. All the way around the ring they slowly trotted. The music stopped and Sidney was able to halt Oakley quicker than the other contestant and she ran for the final crate. She sat and claimed it, so I pronounced her the winner as the audience cheered.

This time sparkling eyes joined her smile as she showed Oakley her blue ribbon. Then the little girl gave the old mare a hug and softly said, "Thank you, Oakley."

Chapter 17

Pony Parties With Petey

Petey was our first small pony that we used for pony rides. When we saw the classified ad for him, it said he was 14 hands and 10 years old. When my husband and I went to look at him, I told them that they had it backwards. He was waist high and his teeth showed that he was in his late teens. I like his mellow attitude and his pinto color. His hooves were long and burrs were in his mane and tail, but once he was cleaned up, he made a pretty picture with a young child.

My son, Josh, was five when he entered Petey in a Pet Contest at the Salisbury Civic Center. The pony wore a tiny Western saddle and bridle, with a blue striped saddle blanket and matching ribbons in his mane and tail. Josh proudly wore his cowboy outfit – suede chaps and vest complete with fringe, boots and a tan cowboy hat. A blue bandana around his neck completed his ensemble. He won a trophy in the miscellaneous category. Petey was the first equine entered in the yearly contest.

Other youngsters also enjoyed the little pinto pony. He and another matching pinto mare, Penny, were favorites for Pony Parties. Often the birthday party for a five-year-old was a Western theme with the children dressed as cowboys and cowgirls. Sometimes the boys carried cap guns with them as they took their turns around the backyard.

"Will the pony mind the noise?" asked a worried mom at one such party. "And what about the flash on my camera? Will it scare him?"

"Let's try him without a rider first," I suggested.

Petey must have been nearly deaf as he continued to graze on their landscaped lawn without flinching when the birthday boy shot his cap gun. Then the camera's flash went off and Petey lifted his head curiously but that was it.

"What a great pony!" My client was impressed and so was I.

After that party, I realized I didn't need to worry about screaming, running children or popping balloons. Petey never paid attention to the odd decorations, even at the school fairs where crepe paper ran rampant. He got along with the comical clowns and the magnificent magicians. All in a day's work for Petey. As long as there was something to eat he was happy. Grass wasn't hard to find, and most often the kids wanted to hand feed apple or carrot pieces.

"Will he bite if the children give him a treat?"

"They need to keep their hands flat and Petey will just tickle their palm as he takes the apple piece. I'll help hold their hands to show them."

I always had the parent cut the treat into small pieces to fit on the little hands. Invariable, the youngsters would pull away at the last minute dropping the treats on the ground. Petey didn't mind if they were a little dirty. With practice, the children were soon shoving carrots and apples into Petey's mouth faster than he could chew. That's why he loved Pony Parties.

For many years, Petey did pony rides at a day care center for their end of season fair. The owner was very organized and she set up four activity areas for her little guests. Petey was one of the activities, and every fifteen minutes a bell would ring signaling the guest to move on to the next activity. About six little ones would enjoy as many rides on Petey as the bell would allow.

One pig-tailed girl wouldn't stop petting Petey's neck every time she had her turn. An obvious horse lover, I called her "Little Sharon" since she reminded me of my own childhood as a horse-crazy kid. Little Sharon reluctantly left when the bell rang but appeared by Petey's side for the last two sessions. She gave me a Mona Lisa smile and I winked at her as I lifted her back in the saddle again. Other adults never said a word and I wasn't about to disappoint Petey's most popular fan.

Several years later, a new riding student asked me on the first day, "Is Petey here?"

"No, I'm sorry. He's in horse heaven now. He was old and tired and now he's in peace. I'm glad you remember him though."

"I rode Petey at the party my daycare center held. That was my first experience with horses. He was so cute and his neck was so soft. I cheated and rode him longer than I was suppose to, but I couldn't help it. Petey began my love affair with horses."

"I remember you! You had pigtails and a shy smile. So, now you want to take lessons?"

"Well, after that experience, I spent several weeks every summer riding at my aunt's farm. This past winter she moved and sold her horses. My parents said I can continue riding. They contacted the daycare center to get your name and number. Even though the owner is retired she still had your information."

"It's wonderful to have you join us. I'm sure Petey is smiling down from heaven because he would remember your soft touch."

The young lady gave me another Mona Lisa smile.

Chapter 18

Sandie the Pink Horse

"What's the name of your pink horse?"

I had just unloaded my four school horses from the trailer and tied them to its side. We were at a small horse show and eight of my riding students were entered in the children's divisions.

"Her name is Sandie. She is a strawberry roan, but she does look pink doesn't she?"

The little girl wearing breeches and paddock boots smiled and nodded as she continued on her way. My riders gathered their grooming tools and worked diligently on cleaning their mounts. I had assigned two riders per horse. One youngster would ride in the short stirrup division and the older child would enter in the junior division.

Sandie was previously a boarder. The teenage girl went off to college and I like the sweet mare so much that I agreed to keep her and use her for lessons in exchange for the board. The girl had shown Sandie locally, so I knew the aged mare wouldn't get flustered at the change of scenery. Beginner students need reliable mounts. The riders are usually nervous at their first show and they don't need a nervous horse.

When Sandie and the other three horses were sparkling clean and tacked up, I had the older children take them to the ring to warm up before the first class began. Sandie marched obediently around the ring next to the rail as directed. She looked around but with a curious glance, not a skittish one.

After the riders walked and trotted both ways without problems, I had the riders switch and then adjusted their stirrups. The younger students would be riding in the early

93

morning classes. I coached them and all four had control and sat in the correct position. When the ring steward announced that the first class would begin in five minutes, I felt my riders were ready.

As we waited outside the ring I gave them last minute advice about following directions and keeping separated. I straightened their numbers to the center of their backs, and wiped off the children's boots and horses' mouths. The Short Stirrup Walk class was announced and I sent them off like a parent does on her child's first day of school.

The class was large with eight riders. Three rode English and the rest, including my beginners, rode Western. Sandie, the only pink horse in the ring, caught the judge's attention each time she went by. Fortunately, my young rider was confident and guided the 15-hand mare close to the rail. She passed slower horses in excellent form as she rode by the judge. All my horses did well but I was not surprised when Sandie won first place. The child beamed as she accepted her blue ribbon.

The same riders stayed in the ring for the Walk/Trot class. Western riders would jog, or do a slower sitting trot. The English riders would post the trot but diagonals would not count except to break a tie. They were asked to walk and then trot or jog as they tracked left around the ring. Then, after walking and changing direction, they were asked to trot or jog the other way.

Sandie tripped and my rider lost her composure for a moment. I was relieved when I noticed the judge had her back to the pair and did not see the misstep. Finally the announcer asked the riders to line up in the center of the ring. Then he asked something my riders weren't prepared for, and neither was I.

"As the judge stands in front of your horse, please ask it to back up three steps, stop, and then walk forward three steps."

All four of my riders looked at me in confusion. It was my fault that they weren't sure what to do. I had not practiced backing at home with them. It was not usually asked of such young riders, but apparently the judge was having difficulty deciding between the riders.

By luck, my riders were lined up at the end. They watched how the first four entries asked their mounts to back. Sandie's turn came next. My confident rider pulled and relaxed the reins just like the previous entries. Like the experienced show horse she was, Sandie dropped her head and took three steps, halted and moved forward on command back to the line. Her young rider smiled at the judge and the judge smiled back. My other horses didn't comply as readily and one horse stepped back in a zigzag motion. Sandie won the blue ribbon again.

For the last class, the riders would negotiate a trail course set up with simple obstacles. The riders had to memorize the course and follow directions, asking their horse to walk or trot where specified. The riders' numbers were called at random. The first few horses were reluctant at some of the obstacles. Most of my riders had a couple of errors.

The final entry was Sandie. As usual, Sandie obediently responded to her rider and did not hesitate walking over the plastic blue tarp or wooden ground poles. She halted quietly at the mailbox for the rider to open the lid and retrieve the newspaper. The mare jogged smoothly to a barrel where the rider placed the paper and circled a cone at a jog without breaking to a walk. She stopped at the finish line and paused for five seconds as requested.

Sandie was the first horse to complete the course without a mistake and the audience broke the silence with a gusty applause. Sandie won that class and was awarded the championship ribbon for the Short Stirrup division.

Next, Sandie and my other horses were entered in the English Pleasure Junior division. We changed the tack and the older riders practiced in the pasture to warm up. I coached them about their diagonals, which would count in this older division. I reminded them about staying at a consistent speed and following the directions announced over the loudspeaker. They practiced cantering on the correct lead and jumping cross rails in their jump seat. They would jump a course of six fences instead of negotiating an obstacle course. I walked the course with them on foot during the allotted time, advising them on strategy.

Sandie did not have the build or color of an English horse. She was stocky with her draft horse background, and her roan coat and flaxen mane and tail contrasted sharply with the bays and chestnuts.

The judge could not fault her steady gaits and smooth jumping style, but it was the rider who was judged anyway, not the horse. Sandie performed perfectly, making her rider look like a winner. Sandie earned her second championship after the junior division finished.

In the early afternoon, adults rode in the pleasure classes and my horses took a break and enjoyed grazing. The last division of the day was the gymkhana. I entered Sandie because that was her specialty with her previous rider. I wanted to see if the old girl still had what it takes to beat the local gaming ponies.

I tacked her up in my Western saddle and signed up for three classes – pole bending, barrel racing and the flag race. When I approached the gate to the first class, Sandie's attitude reverted to her glory days. She pranced and chomped on the bit, ready to go. She knew her job and there was no small child on her now. She was anticipating a good gallop to let off steam.

To the astonishment of the audience and the other competitors, Sandie out-timed all the horses in the three games. But the judge was the most surprised.

"Isn't that the same horse who won this morning with two championships for the children?"

"Yes, it is," I replied as I patted the mare's sweaty neck.

"Wow. What a horse!"

Yes, Sandie was a very special pink horse.

Chapter 19

Riding Bareback With Star

"Who wants to learn to ride bareback today?" I asked my riding students.

"I do! I do!" Four ten-year-old campers chirped their response.

The girls shared a bunk at Lake Bryn Mawr Camp and had requested an "Early Bird" ride. It was August, and the week had been hot, so riding before breakfast when it was cooler was a relief to the horses, staff and riders. After feeding and bringing in the horses, I decided these advanced youngsters were ready to ride without saddles. They had been riding three or more times a week and had secure seats and strong legs. They all eagerly agreed.

The four girls took lessons at home and one owned a show pony. Yet, none had ridden bareback. At the beginning of summer, I always had the riders set goals. Some wanted to learn to canter or jump, while others wanted to try something new that they didn't experience at their stable at home. So I offered vaulting, trail rides and bareback lessons.

"After we groom all the horses I will assign you the one you will ride," I continued. "You will still wear your helmets and the horses will wear their bridles."

"How do we get on without stirrups?" asked Rachel, a bright-eyed camper with long dark hair.

Rachel was the most experienced in the group and was able to mount any horse she was assigned without assistance. She simply lowered the stirrup to the bottom hole and with her thin, long legs she bent herself like a pretzel to climb up. She refused to use the mounting block or be given a "leg up" by the instructor.

99

"I'll show you how to mount bareback when we get to the ring. But you might need to use a mounting block."

When all the horses were groomed I selected four with the most comfortable backs and gaits. I assigned Star to Rachel. She had ridden him a couple of times in the beginning of summer but as her talent became obvious, she was assigned the upper level horses. Rachel was able to jump a three-foot fence and ask a horse to do a flying change of leads.

Star was saved mostly for beginner riders, or sometimes for intermediate ones who were learning to canter and jump vertical fences. The 14.3 hand gelding was a grey but had hair as white as snow except when he had rolled in a mud puddle. He had no white markings so he must have received his name because he was the "star" of the riding program. His smooth gaits were unmatched by any other horse and his calm disposition helped to soothe the most nervous rider. He wasn't as old as some of the other beginner's mounts, so occasionally he was asked to prove his athletic skills.

Star had one fault; he hated when the girth was tightened. The instructors had to make sure the rider was nowhere near Star's mouth when a girth check was done. He would snap at the air and if another horse, or human, stood too close, Star would try to bite the surprised victim. He always wore a fleece girth cover and never had a girth sore while I cared for him, but apparently sometime in his history he experienced pain in that area and never forgot.

The excited riders led their horses to the ring and I demonstrated how to mount without a saddle. I chose Star because I had been on him bareback several times and knew he would stand quietly.

"Hold the reins and mane in your left hand. Jump up and lay your belly over the back and then kick out with your legs like a fish until you can swing your right leg over the rump."

I mounted Star in one smooth motion and then dismounted.

"Okay, Rachel, why don't you try first."

The young girl wasn't as tall as me and on the first attempt, Rachel was unable to lay her belly over Star's back.

"Can I take a running start?"

I agreed, and held Star and stroked his neck. Rachel ran three steps and jumped, this time succeeding. She wiggled her legs until she was able to swing her leg over and sit up.

"I did it!"

The other girls tried but only the one on the smaller pony was able to mount without help. The remaining riders used the mounting block.

I had them walk along the rail to warm up the horses.

"Keep your riding position with your back straight, your knee bent and your heel down. Pretend you have stirrups. That's it. Do you feel the muscles moving underneath you?"

"Yes, this is so cool!" answered Rachel and the other girls agreed.

After reversing direction and walking the other way, I asked if they wanted to trot. They said yes with enthusiasm. All four trotted on the rail and all four were able to post. When it came time to canter, I let Rachel go first. The girls lined up their mounts at one end of the ring.

"I want you to ride the canter like the beginners do on their first try. Walk away from me tracking left, down the long side. About halfway down, do a sitting trot. At the far end, ask the horse to canter using the same aids as you would if you had a saddle. But this time, hold onto the mane with your inside hand. Keep the pressure on the outside rein so your horse stays on the rail. If he turns sharply to go in the middle of the ring, you may lose your balance."

Rachel followed directions perfectly and Star brought her home with a huge smile.

"That was easy," she exclaimed. "Can I go again?"

"Yes, after everyone has their turn."

They were all well balanced at the canter and we still had time before breakfast, so I set up ground poles. They practiced balancing in their jump seat over the poles, laughing when they almost fell off. Soon, they all were secure so I set up a low cross rail after the poles. The horses trotted smooth and steady but only Rachel held her perfect position.

"Can I try jumping Star higher?" asked Rachel as they returned to a walk. "How about a vertical?"

"I'll set up a low one but Star will probably canter over it," I responded.

"That's okay. I can do it."

"Do me a favor and hang onto the mane as you jump, okay?"

The young girl trotted around the ring once to establish a steady pace and then lined Star up for the cavalletti poles. She continued a nice working trot around the ring, heading for the vertical. Sure enough, when he saw the higher jump in front of him, he broke into his slow canter and cleared the fence with room to spare. Rachel hung on as I had requested and landed after the jump in perfect poise.

"That was great!" Rachel patted Star's neck as she walked back to me. Star agreed by blowing his nose in satisfaction.

"Do you other girls want to try?"

They shook their heads, so I let Rachel go one more time before ending the lesson. While they cooled down their horses, Rachel came over to me.

"Thanks so much for letting me jump Star at a canter. I really love bareback!"

"Star loves bareback, too. No girth to tighten!"

Chapter 20

Vaulting on Sonny

"Can I try standing up on Sonny at a walk now?"

Brittany was begging me with her eyes as well as her words. I was teaching a vaulting class at a private girl's school and we had finished the basic compulsory movements at a standstill. Now the five teenagers were practicing their favorite stance at a walk. Only Brittany was brave enough to ask to stand up at a walk, but I wasn't surprised. She was a gutsy fourteen-year-old during her regular riding lessons as well.

"Please? I trust Sonny, and you know he'll be good."

"Yes," I agreed without hesitation. Sonny had been teaching vaulting lessons with me for more than ten years. The bay gelding, fifteen hands tall, was half Arabian with the smoothest gaits and a dependable attitude.

"Just remember to wait until I say 'okay' before you let go of the handle bars and rise. I have to make sure he is steady first. Go ahead into your frog position now, and I'll ask him to walk."

I commanded the aged gelding to walk on the lunge line. As he circled around me, I watch his steps. When he was tracking up consistently, I gave Brittany the signal to go ahead.

"Keep your eyes up, Brittany, and your knees bent as you rise up. That's it. And remember, your back stays straight while your arms are held out. Excellent! How's the weather up there?"

"This is awesome!"

Her enthusiasm was infectious. Soon, one at a time, the other four girls were standing up on the gelding's back while he marched around me.

Over the next couple of months, we continued with vaulting class three times a week, eventually practicing the moves at a trot and canter. Only Brittany dared to try standing at the canter. Her classmates were content to just kneel going that fast.

Several months later, in early spring, Brittany and her friends were ready for a public demonstration. I had organized an open house event that I called, "Horse Fest," which would be held in the indoor ring. The vaulting team would be one of the mounted exhibitions and even the girls' parents would be there. They had picked a red, white and blue theme including their shirts and Sonny's pom-poms in his braided mane and tail. I bought a flag-colored saddle pad for under the vaulting rig. They chose their music – Simon and Garfunkel's Fifty Ninth Street Bridge song – and we were set.

That is, until the morning of the event.

First thing that morning, Brittany was kicked while walking between two horses that were participating in the Parade of Breeds. She went down and was crying in pain, so an ambulance was called. Her mother went with her to the hospital and I didn't expect to see them again until later that evening.

Her teammates were distraught, but I assured them that Brittany would be all right, at worst with a cast on her lower leg. They decided they wanted to continue with their demonstration. They would perform as planned, just skipping Brittany's spot.

When our afternoon time slot approached, the girls finalized their preparations. Sonny adored all the attention as they brushed his bay dappled body and combed his black tail. I tightened the cinch on the vaulting rig and made sure the riding helmets were secured properly.

Then Brittany showed up, dressed in her riding clothes.

"What are you doing here? Aren't you supposed to be in the hospital?"

"She wouldn't stay," explained her mother. "The doctor said it was just a bad bruise and nothing was broken."

"I had an ice pack on it all day," continued Brittany. "I didn't practice all these months just to sit it out now."

I looked at her mother. "Are you okay with this?"

"Brittany insisted. She promised that after the show she would follow the doctor's advice and elevate her leg."

"I'm okay," insisted the teenager. "Really. I trust Sonny. Let's go, they just announced us."

As we walked through the gate to the indoor arena, I whispered to Brittany. "Don't try standing at a trot or canter if the motion is too much for your leg. Just stay in the frog position."

She nodded but had a determined smile that made me think she was going to go all out, and would put on the performance of her life.

The morning sprinkles changed to a steady rainfall. I made introductions to the audience with the microphone and explained briefly about vaulting.

"Once an Olympic sport, vaulting is a great confidence builder as well as a fun riding activity. It's like gymnastics on horseback, but with the balance beam moving in a large circle. Vaulting off the horse while in motion helps to prevent the fear of falling."

I explained the compulsory moves as each girl mounted and performed them at a standstill. Sonny, familiar to crowds at horse shows, took all the clapping in stride.

The music was turned on as the team began demonstrating their skills at a walk and trot. All went well, with Sonny only shying once when a flashbulb went off near his face. Fortunately, the girl was still holding the handlebars on the vaulting rig and was not unbalanced.

When Brittany's turn came to stand at the trot, she glanced at me and smiled as she let go and rose up in perfect form. As she vaulted off and landed on her hands and knees, I knew she must be in pain. Bravely, she stood and walked back in line to wait for her next turn, with only a slight limp.

The audience was amazed as the girls performed at a trot, but even more so at the canter. Sonny began to pick up speed as the clapping became intense. I whispered to each girl just before they vaulted on to wait until I nodded before letting go of the rig. As the lively music repeated, I spoke softly to Sonny to get his attention and settle him down. When he was cantering smoothly, I gave the signal and the girls each performed flawlessly. Brittany was last, and despite my warnings about Sonny's speed, she insisted she was going to try to stand.

I could sense the audience holding their breath as Brittany concentrated on the rhythm while crouched in the frog position. Sonny's canter steadied as he blew his nose in contentment. Brittany looked up, let go of the handlebars of the vaulting rig and rose, keeping her knees bent. Her arms were outstretched and she smiled ear to ear. The audience seemed to understand the difficulty in this endeavor and the only thing I could hear was the final notes of Simon and Garfunkel.

Brittany did a smooth dismount and the clapping drowned out the rain on the roof.

"I told you Sonny would be a good boy!"

"Yes, Brittany. You're right. Sonny's a very good boy."

As the teenager patted him and gave him apple pieces, I told her, "And you weren't so bad yourself."

Epilogue

"A horse! A horse! My kingdom for a horse!"
From *King Richard III* by William Shakespeare.

There were numerous lesson horses with endearing qualities that I had the pleasure of teaching with, but these are the unique ones that stand out in my memory. Over the past 30 years, I've taught four-year-olds to grandmothers. Each student, and each four-legged partner, has taught me life lessons of confidence, patience and determination to reach one's goal. But mostly, I've learned the wonderment of horses and the pleasures they bestow upon on us humans.

Covers:

Designed by graphic artist, Joshua Miner of Philadelphia, the covers feature Windfield Farewell with Sara on the front cover and Joe on the back at Farewell's retirement home, Apple Brook Farm in central New Jersey.

Artist:

Martina Davidova grew up in Prague, in the Czech Republic. She first came to the United States in her senior year and attended a Pittsburgh area high school where she loved her art classes. She had such a positive experience in the United States that it compelled her to attend the Art Institute, first in Pittsburgh and then in Philadelphia. She graduated with a Bachelor's degree in graphic design.

Martina plans to pursue her master degree and is currently working on her portfolio. This is the first book to publish her sketches.

Martina is an avid animal lover and also enjoys nature, books and movies.

About the Author

Besides being a professional horsewoman for more than 30 years, Sharon Miner has been a published author and freelance writer since 1990 when her first article on Jack Russell Terriers was published in Dog Fancy magazine. She graduated from the Institute of Children's Literature and her young adult novel, *The Delmarva Conspiracy*, was published by Greene Bark Press, Bridgeport, CT, in 1993.

Sharon wrote as a field correspondent for the *News Eagle* and the *Wayne Independent*, local newspapers covering Wayne and Pike Counties in PA, from 1997 - 2000. She was creator and editor of *Stable News*, a bi-monthly publication that was published in 1997 and later sold to *Horse News*. Since 1997, she has been a freelance writer for *Horse News*, an equine publication covering the horse industry in Pennsylvania and New Jersey. She has had numerous articles published in *Trenton Times, Scranton Times, Pocono Record*, and other local newspapers. Recently, she's had horse articles published in *Blood Horse* and *Mid-Atlantic Thoroughbred Breeders* magazines. She is also the editor for the *Pennsylvania Equine Council's* newsletter and state directory.

Sharon is a member of the Society of Children's Book Writers and Illustrators (SCBWI), Certified Horsemanship Association (CHA), and the Pennsylvania Equine Council (PEC).

Visit the Web sites at:

www.scbwi.org
www.cha-ahse.org
www.pennsylvaniaequinecouncil.com
www.HorseNewsOnline.com
www.bloodhorse.com
www.greenebarkpress.com

Other Books by Sharon Miner

■ *The Delmarva Conspiracy*

A teenager learns about the history of the Holocaust and the meaning of true courage when his family uncovers a secret Neo-Nazi plot to take over the Delmarva Peninsula. This young adult adventure novel is geographically and historically accurate, and horses are used in the rescue scene.

■ *Octavia's Quest*

Octavia Vintara is a ninth-grade social studies teacher at Masonville High School in a small northeastern Pennsylvania town. Her personal mission is to deter her young cousin and other at-risk teenagers from a permanent life of crime. Octavia's father, Lieutenant Gordon Vintara, a soon-to-retire police detective, agrees to become involved with his daughter's plan. Gordon, who had been recently injured while on duty, is assigned a desk job: to reopen cold murder cases. Together, they involve Octavia's class in the details of a thirty-year old murder, hoping to inspire the teens as they attempt to solve the mystery that involves a neglected young boy. The teenagers discover the truth about the murder and also about false assumptions. To be published in Spring 2005.

Octavia's Quest is one of a series of murder mysteries featuring Octavia Vintara, her class and Lieutenant Gordon Vintara.

■ *Beloved School Horses – From Around the Country*

Volume II will feature special school horses from riding stables located in a variety of states. Sharon interviewed instructors about horses that were near and dear to the hearts of their riders. If you have a story to share, please contact the author. To be published in Fall 2005.

■ *Where's Mom?*

Lisa Van Scoy, housewife and mother of five children, on a ski vacation in the Pocono is carjacked in a parking lot.

In Philadelphia, 120 miles away, Lisa awakens with amnesia. An eccentric old woman, Nikki, discovers Lisa and takes her in, introducing her to various patrons of St. Anne's shelter where Nikki works. There, Lisa finds peace and true friends.

The story develops uniquely, through different characters' point of views in each chapter. The reader is drawn in by the question, does she or doesn't she remember her past? Does Lisa remember and just not want to return? Is her new life so much more rewarding that she denies the existence of her real family?

Excitement builds to the climax when she is confronted with a plea from her family in the form of a Web site found on the Internet. Publishing date TBA.

For More Information Visit:

www.sharonminer.com

To Order Signed Copies, Contact the Author at:

sharonminer@yahoo.com

or

Sharon Miner

5992D Steubenville Pike, PMB#203

McKees Rocks, PA 15136